SECRETS YOU NEVER KNEW
ABOUT
STOCK MARKET INVESTING
AND **TRADING**

SECRETS YOU NEVER KNEW
ABOUT
STOCK MARKET INVESTING
AND **TRADING**

Earn more by doing less in the
stock market.

**SWAMINATHAN
ANNAMALAI**

PARTRIDGE

Copyright © 2018 by Swaminathan Annamalai.

ISBN: Softcover   978-1-5437-0196-8
        eBook   978-1-5437-0197-5

All rights reserved. No part of this book may be used or reproduced by any means, graphic, electronic, or mechanical, including photocopying, recording, taping or by any information storage retrieval system without the written permission of the author except in the case of brief quotations embodied in critical articles and reviews.

Because of the dynamic nature of the Internet, any web addresses or links contained in this book may have changed since publication and may no longer be valid. The views expressed in this work are solely those of the author and do not necessarily reflect the views of the publisher, and the publisher hereby disclaims any responsibility for them.

Print information available on the last page.

To order additional copies of this book, contact
Partridge India
000 800 10062 62
orders.india@partridgepublishing.com

www.partridgepublishing.com/india

TO MY FAMILY

ACKNOWLEDGEMENTS

First of all I would like to thank my family for supporting me in my desire to follow my dreams.

Special thanks to my father, Mr. A. Swaminathan, for trusting me and allowing me to be his portfolio manager at a very young age.

My eternal gratitude to my mother, Late Mrs. S. Meenakshi, for teaching me what it is to love and to dream. She instilled in me the values of hard work and perseverance. I owe what I am today, to my parents.

Thanks to my close friend, Mr. N. Kumar, for encouraging me to cultivate and pursue the habit of reading. "You become the books you read," says a popular proverb - this is true in my case. I have learnt that the moment we stop learning, we stop growing.

Thanks to authors Mr. Robin Sharma and T. T. Rangarajan for changing my attitude towards life - through their books.

Thanks to Mr. Gerry Roberts for teaching me how to become an author. The techniques he taught helped me write this book.

Thanks to Mr. M. Kishore for teaching me the less known facts about the stock market. I believe such information is indeed wealth.

Thanks to Mr. Abishek Antony for designing the business logo and website.

Thanks to Ms. Ashika Kumar for proofreading the manuscript.

Thanks to the entire team of Partridge Publications for guiding me through the publication process and publishing the book on time.

Last, but not the least, a big thanks to my children for being my motivation during tough times. The difficulties I face seem to disappear the moment I see them. I've taken long breaks from writing this book, but watching my daughter do her homework has many a times inspired me to finish a pending chapter or start a new one. My children have motivated me to bring this book to fruition and now, it has been published.

PURPOSE OF THIS BOOK

When I started searching for books related to the Indian stock market, I realized that there are either books that deal with a lot of technical material like charting and formulae - which a layman cannot understand; or there are books that provide information about very old share market data, which is of no use today.

Which is why this book, which is focused solely on the Indian stock market, is the need of the hour.

Many people, without knowing the basics, jump into the stock market to generate passive income and burn their hands. This book is my sincere attempt to simplify the complicated subject of stock market. It is written in a simple manner such that even someone with basic qualifications and without any prior financial knowledge can easily understand the concepts.

This book is aimed at smart short-term traders and wise investors; but, that doesn't mean this book is not for intraday traders; I want intraday traders to read this book and be inspired to begin short-term trading and investing.

Many stock market legends around the world, like Mr. Warren Buffet, have become wealthy by investing and not by trading intraday. Remember, by trading intraday it is your broker who gets richer, not you.

You don't need to be an analyst to earn consistently in the stock market. By investing in quality stocks at the right time anyone who is not greedy can earn well in the stock market.

WHY THIS BOOK IS A MUST READ?

This book opens doors to learning more about the following:

1. Earn money without sitting in front of the computer all day during market hours.
2. Identify multi baggers at an early stage and reap maximum profit.
3. Tackling delisted shares that are not traded in the stock exchange.
4. Selling naked options and increasing your chances of winning.
5. Information about IPO and how to get IPO funding.
6. Dematerialising physical shares.
7. The low-down on what BeES is and if it is a safe investment option.
8. Introduction to stock screeners.

9. Different types of scams to impact the stock market.
10. Saving income tax by forming a HUF.

Packed with practical and easy to follow advice, everything is explained in simple language. This book is all you need to make a fortune out of the stock market, in a relaxed way.

ABOUT THE AUTHOR

Swaminathan Annamalai is an NISM certified research analyst. He completed his Masters in Computer & Information Networks from University of Essex, UK. He began trading and investing in the Indian stock market during his undergraduate days and through the income generated from investing, he was able to take care of his own expenses. Through consistent stock trading, he was able to become financially free - i.e., the passive income he generated was much more than his expenses.

Despite being a successful businessman, he realized that irrespective of your profession, you must have at least one steady source of passive income; and the stock market perfectly fits that bill, because, when done right, it is one of the best places to earn a consistent passive income in a relaxed way.

The author's curiosity of the stock market led him to learn about it even as a child. Mr. Warren Buffet became an inspiration to him. He began attending seminars and reading books about stock market and stock market legends. The more he learnt, the more he began to fall in love with the stock market and it became his passion.

His journey began when the author's father enlisted his help to exchange all his physical shares in the dematerialised format (because of SEBI's rule about trading in the dematerialised format). He is indebted to his father for this, because what began as a simple gesture of helping his father transformed into a deep learning experience where he fell in love with the stock market and now, eighteen years later, has gained enough knowledge and experience to write a book about it.

The author lives in Chennai with his wife, Alamu, daughter Meenal and son Arjun Saminathann. Apart from spending his time trading shares, the author loves to travel, indulge in nature and plays chess.

Follow the author at:
https://www.facebook.com/equityforte
https://www.instagram.com/equityforte
https://www.twitter.com/equityforte

www.equityforte.com

About equityforte.com

Equityforte.com is a one-stop shop for all your needs; be it dematerialization of shares, unclaimed dividends, selling delisted shares, reviewing existing portfolio as well as offering investment advice. Our service is custom designed and each case is thoroughly researched and the solutions offered are unique to each issue.

Equityforte.com acts as a bridge between you and the respective companies to resolve any issues. Your case is taken up with the pertaining authorities and as soon as we enter an agreement your hassle becomes ours; we take over all the legwork and frustrations associated with lengthy legal procedures. You can rest assured that we will not leave any stone unturned and walk every extra mile to ensure that your rightful money returns to you.

Not only do we operate on a policy of utter transparency, we also provide competitive rates. Our trades are genuine and we guarantee completed deals with absolutely no hidden charges. We even provide unique exit routes to those who are stuck with sizeable quantities of delisted securities that they are unable to sell.

Our mission is to create tangible value for your blocked investments and provide exceptional service while continually raising our standards of excellence. We aim to not only meet, but also exceed the expectations of our clients. Our clients profit is our motto and our priority.

For any further queries feel free to drop us an email at contact@equityforte.com

DISCLAIMER

The information/content (including any tables/pictures) in this book has been compiled from sources we believe to be true and reliable, but we do not hold ourselves responsible for its completeness or accuracy. Any omissions/errors are accidental and not intentional. This is not an offer to sell or solicitation to buy any securities in any jurisdiction. Author will not be liable for any losses incurred or investment(s) made or decisions taken/or not taken based on the information provided in this book. Before acting on any information/recommendation, readers should consider whether it is suitable for their particular circumstances and, if necessary, seek professional advice. Author may not hold any securities mentioned herein and may from time to time, have a relationship with any company reported in this book in the ordinary course of business. All opinions/views, if any, are subject to change from time to time without notice.

All rights reserved. Any act of copying, reproducing or distributing the contents of this book whether wholly or in part, for any purpose without the permission of the author is strictly prohibited and shall be deemed to be copyright infringement.

CONTENTS

1. ABC of Equities and Stock Market............ 1

- ➢ Introduction 1
- ➢ Three-in-one account..................................3
- ➢ What you need to open a three-in-one account? 5
- ➢ How to select a stock broker? 5
- ➢ Benefits of equity investing 6
- ➢ Risks involved in equity investing 7
- ➢ How Much Risk Is Right for You? 8
- ➢ Cost of equity investment 9
- ➢ Know your contract note 10
- ➢ Purpose of the contract note 11
- ➢ Why stock market investment is a must for everyone?...................................12

2. Secrets For Wise Investors 13

- ➢ Cyclical companies 13
- ➢ Non-cyclical companies 14
- ➢ Three phases of rally 15

- Diversified portfolio 17
- Time your investment 17
- Bonus 22
- Stock Split 23
- Rights Issue 24
- Buyback of shares 25
- Dividends 26
- Nifty BeES 29
- Various criteria for a stock to be included in the index: 32
- Different types of BeES 33
- The quarterly result of a company - what to see & what to ignore? 35
- Global economic factors that can affect your portfolio 36
- Stock screener 37
- What is alpha and beta of a stock and why is it important? 39
- Key parameters to keep in mind while analyzing various sectors 41
- Scam 45
- How to choose a stock advisor? 49
- Why not mutual funds? 50
- Stocks to avoid when it comes to investment ... 52
- Misconceptions 55
- Dos & Don'ts 55

3. Secrets for Smart Traders............................ 57

- ➢ Why is the term "Stop loss" famous with intraday traders? 58
- ➢ Common mistakes that intraday traders make: 61
- ➢ Chart Based Trading............................63
- ➢ News based trading.............................. 64
- ➢ Futures...65
- ➢ Position Trading Technique 67
- ➢ Stock maximiser technique 70
- ➢ Standard & Poor's 500 Index - S&P 500 futures..72
- ➢ Options..74
- ➢ Naked options writing 77
- ➢ Why writing options has a higher winning probability? 78
- ➢ Difference between futures and options: 83

4. IPO (Initial Public Offering) 84

- ➢ Three categories of investors:.........................86
- ➢ What is meant by oversubscribed?................87
- ➢ Dos & Don'ts
- ➢ Pros and Cons of an IPO 89
- ➢ What is 'ASBA'?..90
- ➢ Advantage an investor has in applying through ASBA..93
- ➢ IPO funding..94
- ➢ Pros and Cons of IPO funding 96

5. Dematerialisation 98

- ➢ What is a Demat Account? 100
- ➢ Dematerialisation 100
- ➢ Step by step procedure to dematerialise physical shares 101
- ➢ Most common reasons for demat rejection 106
- ➢ Special Cases
- ➢ How to find the transfer agent of a particular company? 110
- ➢ Advantages of dematerialisation 110

6. Delisting 113

- ➢ Voluntary delisting 113
- ➢ Compulsory delisting 114
- ➢ The Nasty Side of Delisting 115
- ➢ How to sell shares that are not traded anymore? 117
- ➢ Why a dealer purchases delisted shares? 117

7. Hindu Undivided Family (HUF): a Less Known Tax Saving Tool 120

- ➢ HUF (Hindu Undivided Family) 120
- ➢ MEMBERS OF HUF 121
- ➢ How to create an HUF? 121
- ➢ HOW TO CREATE HUF CAPITAL? 123
- ➢ Different sources of income permitted to be shown under HUF 124

- ➤ Tax benefits on a HUF account: 125
- ➤ How to save tax by forming HUF?............125
- ➤ OTHER RELEVANT POINTS
  REGARDING HUF...............................127
- ➤ Disadvantages of HUF account 128
- ➤ Conclusion..129

8. Famous Quotes by Legends 130

- ➤ Warren Buffet quotes: 130
- ➤ Rakesh Jhunjhunwala quotes 134
- ➤ Peter Lynch quotes....................................136
- ➤ Benjamin Graham quotes 137
- ➤ Brian Tracy...138
- ➤ Philip Fisher quotes...................................139
- ➤ Stephen Covey quotes 140

CHAPTER 1

ABC of Equities and Stock Market

Many people see the stock market as a casino and the people involved as gamblers. But the stock market is the best way to generate consistent passive income in a relaxed way. With the technology available today, one can easily monitor the stock market from any part of the world - even on a smart phone.

In today's world, having a second source of income is not just desirable, but also necessary; however, it's not always possible or even easy. In such a case, the stock market presents itself as an excellent option. Make the stock market work for you and don't avoid it because of fear or frustration.

This book is for those who are new to the stock market as well as for those with many years of experience.

Bruce Lee rightly said, "Empty your cup, so that it may be filled". Prepare to unlearn and relearn. Empty your minds of all your previous stock market knowledge and refill it with information that truly works.

Those involved in the stock market can be classified into three categories:

- ➢ Intraday traders
- ➢ Short-term traders
- ➢ Long -term investors

Intraday traders

Intraday traders are those who open (buys) and close (sells) a position in a security, in the same trading day. Usually these traders have very little capital or they trade with borrowed money. They are involved in trading throughout market hours and they try to enter and close as many trades as possible.

Long-term investors

Investors buys stocks with the intention of holding on to them for more than a year. They invest in high-quality stocks that they mostly buy and rarely sell. They reap profits through price appreciation, dividends, bonuses and share splits.

Short-term traders

Short-term traders open and close a position in a security within a year. They get into a trade very patiently and get out very aggressively. Most of the smart short-term traders rely on charts to enter/exit a trade and rely on news to pick a stock from a particular sector.

Three-in-one account

Stock trading requires three different accounts:

- A bank account to send and receive money.
- A trading account to place your buy/sell orders.
- A demat account to hold the shares in an electronic format.

Any one can open a three-in-one account with a bank. A three-in-one account is convenient and works as a single integrated savings, demat and trading account.

Why get a three-in-one account?

- The transfer of funds from your savings to trading account is just a click away.
- The funds transfer is secure because money can only be transferred between linked trading and savings accounts.
- No need to remember multiple login details.

- Any IPO application through ASBA (Application Supported by Blocked Amount) is convenient, saves time and avoids paper work. (Discussed in detail in Chapter 4).
- Dividends automatically get credited to the linked bank account.

Why choose your bank as your broker, rather than a standalone firm?

Choose your bank as the broker and avoid standalone brokerage firms for the following reasons:

- Banks have money readily available than a standalone brokerage firm and can sustain big blows during a market crash. Your money is always safer with a bank than with standalone brokerage firm.
- Standalone brokerage firms are not trustworthy because they can easily shutdown and run away with the money in your trading account.
- As per Securities and Exchange Board of India (SEBI) regulations, funds left in the trading account should be returned to the savings account periodically. Fresh funds need to be allocated for purchasing new shares at a later date; if your trading account and bank account are with two different entities, transferring money between accounts takes more time.

What you need to open a three-in-one account?

Anyone who wants to open a three-in-one account has to submit the following documents:

- Proof of identity – e.g. PAN card, passport.
- Proof of residence – e.g. driving license, ration card.
- Passport size photos.
- A cheque from any one of your personal accounts.
- Aadhar card.
- Completed and signed application form.

How to select a stock broker?

Most traders look for brokers who charge the least commission. The brokerage fee is an important criterion, but not at the cost of service. Prioritize the stockbroker's services over the cost; take into account the stockbroker's reputation, accessibility and quality of service before choosing the right one for you.

A good stockbroker should provide the following services:

- A robust online trading platform for both desktop and mobile.
- The broker's website should provide all the reports in downloadable format (excel or pdf), required for income tax filing.

- Transparency - make sure that the stockbroker has displayed brokerage and other charges (like security transaction tax, service tax, depository charges) on his website. Be sure that there are no hidden costs.
- Quality Customer Support - online chat, email and phone support for trading related queries or account related queries is a must.
- Trading Tools - consider a broker who can give features like Aftermarket Order (AMO), Valid Till Cancel (VTC) and other useful trading tools. We'll discuss these in detail in the coming chapters.
- Look for a broker who can provide maximum uptime with the stock exchange without any interruptions.

Benefits of equity investing

The benefits a shareholder will enjoy can be classified into two categories:

- Monetary benefits.
- Non-monetary benefits.

Monetary benefits

A shareholder will get the following monetary benefits:

- Dividend - companies distribute profits to shareholders - in part or in full - through dividends.

- Capital Appreciation - shareholders benefit from capital appreciation. When the company performs well, its share price automatically increases.

Non-monetary benefits

A shareholder will get the following non-monetary benefits:

- Bonus - companies issue bonus shares free of cost instead of distributing accumulated profits.
- Rights issue - a rights issue is an invitation to existing shareholders to purchase additional new shares in the company.

Risks involved in equity investing

Although equity investing is rewarding, one should be aware of the risks involved.

Political risk
There is always the possibility of a country's government suddenly changing its policies. Events such as wars and unfavorable economic policies can adversely impact the financial markets.

Economic risk
The risk that the economy, as a whole, will suffer a downturn. Such an event usually affects the stock market negatively.

Industry risks
The risk that a specific industry will suffer a downturn; this in turn will affect the stock of those industries.

Liquidity risk
The risk of not being able to sell your shares at a fair price; sometimes an investor is unable to convert the equity into cash without giving up capital and/or income due to a lack of buyers or an inefficient market.

Inflation risk
Inflation erodes the purchasing power of money over time – the same amount of money will buy fewer goods and services. Share prices also rise in line with inflation.

Horizon risk
Sometimes your investment horizon gets shortened because of an unforeseen event; hospitalization of a family member, for instance, can cause unexpected expenses. This may force you to sell the shares you were expecting to hold for the long term, in a bear market.

How Much Risk Is Right for You?

When you invest in bank fixed deposits or post office schemes, you are a lender; which means that the risk is low. Whereas, when you invest in equity, real estate or gold you become an owner; owning something always comes with more risk. Hence there should be a balance between both.

A person's risk comfort level depends on the following factors:

Investment objective - one must know their primary objective behind investing. For some it could be creating wealth and for some it may be a second source of income.

Investment horizon - how long you can wait to reap the benefits? The longer you stay invested, the higher are the chances of getting good returns.

Age - creating wealth requires time and capital. Risk taking mentality generally decreases with age; so it's better to begin investing when you're young.

Family situation - based on the number of dependents you have, your risks should be cautious and calculated. Risk taking mentality should be always inversely proportion to the number of dependents you have.

Income and wealth - a person who has plenty of accumulated wealth and a strong monthly income can take more risks.

Cost of equity investment

When you buy a share you pay the following charges:

- Brokerage – this is the fee that stockbroker's charge for the service they offer; each broker has their own brokerage model.

- Service tax - a flat tax percentage on brokerage is charged for every transaction.
- Securities transaction tax - this refers to the tax payable on the value of securities transacted through a recognized stock exchange. The percentage varies for intraday, delivery, futures and options.
- Turnover tax.
- Stamp duty - stamp duty on securities transactions is the tax levied on documentation by the State Government of India. Stamp duty varies from state to state.

When you sell a share you pay the following taxes:

- All the above-mentioned taxes that you pay when you buy a share.
- Demat transaction charges.
- Capital gain tax when you make a profit.

Know your Contract Note

A contract note is a legal record of any trade carried out on the stock exchange. It acts as a confirmation of trade, for a particular time, on behalf of a client. Nowadays, stockbrokers automatically send this document to their client's registered email in a digitally signed electronic format.

The Contract Note contains the following details:

1. The stockbroker's SEBI registration number.
2. Settlement number and Contract Note number.
3. Contact details & Permanent Account Number (PAN) of the client.
4. Client code.
5. Order number and time.
6. Trade number and time.
7. Name and symbol of the security traded.
8. International Securities Identification Numbers (ISIN).
9. Whether it was a buy or sell action.
10. Quantity traded.
11. Traded price.
12. Brokerage amount.
13. Security Transaction Tax (STT) and service tax on brokerage.
14. Digital signature in electronic format.

Purpose of the Contract Note

A contract note shows:

- Details of brokerage charged.
- Information used to calculate profit/loss when you file income tax.
- Can be used as legal proof in case of any dispute.

Why stock market investment is a must for everyone?

- By buying the shares of a company, you can become the partner of the company without actually owning the business.
- Anyone with a demat, trading and savings account can invest any amount in the stock market.
- Dividends received from any domestic company - of up to Rs.10,00,000 annually - are tax free.
- By just using a smart phone or laptop you can monitor your stock portfolio easily from any part of the world.

The roller-coaster movements of the stock market make most people nervous, but some simple rules can make the ride more comfortable. We'll discuss these simple rules in the coming chapters.

CHAPTER 2

Secrets For Wise Investors

Investing in a company's share is like buying a portion of that company. Before going further, one should know that there are two types of companies:

Cyclical companies

Non-Cyclical companies

Cyclical companies

A cyclical company's share price is directly proportional or related to economic conditions. Sale of these companies will grow when people have more income to spend on luxuries, and will decline when the economy slumps. These companies produce things we can live without when money is tight.

Eg: A common man has to plan his finances to buy a luxury car whereas he never plans finances for daily needs products. Everyone postpones buying luxury products if the economy is not good. Good examples of a cyclical industry are flight travel, holiday and fine dining.

Non-cyclical companies

Economic conditions do not affect the stock prices of non-cyclical companies as they deal with necessary goods and services; their sales are consistent and they are able to make profits regardless of economic conditions.

Cyclical companies	**Non cyclical companies**
Share price fluctuates based on economic conditions.	Share price is not related to economic conditions and hence these are called defensive stocks.
Rally in stock price will last for a short period.	Rally in stock price will last longer.
These companies deal with luxury goods and services.	These companies deal with goods and services that we need on a daily basis.
Sectors like automobile, hotel and airline come under this category.	Sectors like FMCG, pharmaceuticals and power come under this category.

These stocks are a good bet for short term trading. Eg: car, travel, fine dining, etc.	These stocks are a good bet for investing. Eg: soap, medicine, gas, etc.

In conclusion, avoid cyclical companies when it comes to investment.

Three phases of rally

Every good stock has to undergo the following three phases:

- Build up phase
- Prime phase
- Mature phase

Build up phase

Identifying a good stock for investment in this phase is very difficult because:

- The stock would have been an ignored sector or sub-sector for the past two or three years.
- There will be zero or very minimal buy recommendation from analysts.
- P.E ratio will be historically low.

- Promoters of the company will buy or gradually expand existing capacity.

Prime phase

This is the ideal phase to invest. In this phase the stock will slowly show up in the media. Identifying a good stock for investment in this phase is quite possible because:

- It will have a story.
- One can get information about it by keeping a close watch on news every day.
- The most prominent indicator will be that the stock will rise even in a falling market.

Mature phase

Identifying the stock for investment becomes easy in this phase; but one should double check if there is any opportunity for further upward price movement.

- The stock will have many buy recommendations from analysts and copious amounts of media coverage.
- Before picking the stock, first find out whether the story is short-lived or long-lived.
- If the stock is a cyclical company, it's better to not invest in this phase. For a non-cyclical company, there is still possibility for more returns.

Diversified portfolio

A proper diversified portfolio must have limited number of stocks, but be diversified across sectors. By investing in different sectors one can reduce the overall investment risk; also, the poor performance of a single stock or sector will not affect the portfolio's performance.

Remember, no single sector can dominate for long; so there are no permanent winners or losers. The best performing sector of the previous year can become the worst performing sector in the coming years.

Time your investment

Don't invest all your money on a single day - invest gradually. As Warren Buffet said, "It's far better to buy a wonderful company at a fair price than a fair company at a wonderful price."

After choosing the stock and sector to invest in, wait for the right time to buy; don't be in a hurry. Remember, buying a right stock at the wrong price is not a good investment.

"Price is what you pay. Value is what you get." – Warren Buffet

For information on the right timing refer to Nifty PE, because it shows where the market is heading. This information can be acquired from www.nseindia.com.

The following nifty P.E data will let you know when to invest?

If nifty p.e is

<15	Best opportunity to invest 100%
15-18	Stay invested 100%
18-20	Nifty mostly trades in this range. Gradually build the portfolio.
20-22	Be cautious in selecting stocks.
22-24	Market will fall by more than 10% or earnings will expand.
24+	Better not to invest; book profit or wait
25+	One can expect 20% to 30% crash. Sit in cash to re-enter at a low price.

Percentage allocation

A good diversified portfolio should have a maximum of ten to fifteen stocks diversified across five to seven sectors. Allocate a minimum of seven percent and a maximum of fifteen percent per stock. Build your portfolio gradually and stay invested for long to reap all the benefits.

Few examples of a wise investment

Many people succeed in choosing the right stock/sector at a fair price. But they get easily tempted to sell when they see a price rise of ten to fifteen percent. By selling a stock too early you can't reap all the benefits. Staying invested in a good company for a long period will produce unimaginable returns. Let's see this in detail:

Example 1 - MRF

In 2013 the stock price of MRF was approximately Rs.11,000/ share. Many investors would not have invested because of the price tag. To everyone's surprise MRF touched an all time high of approximately Rs. 74,000/share in the year 2017. It has grown to almost 6.7 times the original price – i.e. a 670% increase in just 4 years.

The stock price shot up for the following reasons:

- Cost of rubber decreased.
- Even though the demand for tyres kept on increasing, the selling price of the tyres did not come down.

Example 2 - Ajanta Pharma

In 2013 the stock price of Ajanta Pharma was approximately Rs. 200/ share. Many investors ignored this less known pharma stock. To everyone's surprise Ajanta Pharma touched an all time high of approximately Rs. 1,997/share in the year 2017. It had grown to almost 10 times the original price; i.e. 1000% increase in just four years.

Example 3 - Eicher Motors

Eicher Motors manufactures commercial vehicles like trucks, tractors and owns the famous motorbike brand – Royal Enfield.

One Royal Enfield Bullet was priced at around Rs. 54,000 in 2001. Instead of buying a bullet if a person had invested the same amount in Eicher Motors' stock, then his worth would have been close to Rs. 4.65 crores in 2015.

Unbelievable! In fourteen years, an investment of Rs.54,000 could have turned to Rs 4.65 crores.

Example 4 - Infosys

In 1993, when Infosys went public, if you had invested Rs.10,000 you would have gotten around 100 shares of the company. Until 2015 Infosys announced bonus about seven times and they went for a stock split once. Now, the 100 shares have converted to 46,400 shares. In 2015 the stock was quoted at Rs.1020 per share, which means the investment would now be worth Rs. 4.73 crores. In addition to this, investors got a dividend of approximately Rs. 27 lakhs.

Example 5 -Wipro

If you had invested Rs.10,000 in Wipro in 1980 you would have gotten about 100 shares of the company. Until 2010 Wipro announced bonuses about ten times and they went for a stock split twice. The 100 shares would have converted to 96,00,000 shares. In 2014 the stock was quoted at Rs.555 per share, which means the investment would be worth Rs. 532 crores. In addition to this, investors got a dividend of approximately Rs. 6 crores.

Conclusion

Don't invest in past multibaggers blindly. The examples above are for educational purposes only and I don't recommend readers to buy at the current market price. Most of the investors don't feel satisfied even at a thirty percent increase in their investment. They don't have the patience to hold an appreciated stock in a volatile market. Most of them sell the winners first and hold on to the losers for a long time.

But, if you really want extraordinary returns, you have to do lot of fundamental research on the company and invest in it when it's in the early stages. Identifying high quality stocks is an art and it cannot be mastered quickly. Start building your portfolio slowly and learn from your mistakes. Record your trades in a separate workbook and analyze the reasons for winning and losing. My suggestion is that if you are new to the stock market, don't trade with real money; instead, begin your trade experience with virtual money.

Corporate actions

Following are the different corporate actions that one should know as an investor.

- Bonus
- Stock split
- Rights issue
- Buy back
- Dividend

Generally, all corporate actions are initiated by the board of directors and approved by the company's shareholders through voting.

Bonus

Bonus shares are issued out of the cash reserves of the company. These are like appreciatory gifts to the shareholders for staying invested in the company. An investor gets free shares against the shares that he currently holds. All the investors are allotted bonus shares in a fixed ratio.

Example

Company X allots bonus shares in the ratio of 2:1.

This means that for each share the investor holds, he will get two more shares at no extra cost with same face value. So, if you hold 1000 shares of a company (say current market price is Rs.12) and the company declares a bonus at 2:1 ratio, you will get an extra 2000 shares and the total number of shares you hold will increase to 3000 shares leaving the face value unchanged.

But, remember that it's only the number of shares that increase, though the value of the investment remains the same. After the bonus shares are credited, the price per share will go down according to the ratio. Hence the price falls from Rs.12 to Rs.4.

1000 nos.*12 Rs =Rs.12,000 (before bonus)

3000 nos.*4 Rs = Rs.12,000 (after bonus)

Investment value remains the same and the investor gets free shares of the same face value.

Stock Split

The stock is split in terms of face value. After a stock split, the number of shares held increases and the value of the investment remains the same.

Example

Company X announces 5:1 stock split ratio for a share that has a face value of Rs.10. So, the face value is now split into five parts - new face value becomes 10/5=Rs.2. Since the face value has now decreased to Rs. 2, the current price of the stock adjusts proportionately too.

An investor having fifty nos. at a market price of Rs.100 will have 250 nos. at a price of Rs.20 after stock split

50 nos*100 Rs =Rs.5,000 (before split face value was 10)

250 nos*20 Rs = Rs.5,000 (after split face value will be 2)

The investment value remains the same and the investor receives additional quantity of shares with new face value.

Rights Issue

Rights issue is limited to the existing shareholders and is not for general public. Instead of going for FPO (Further Public Offer), companies use this as an alternative to raise fresh capital from existing shareholders. Generally, the rights issue is offered at a discounted rate to benefit existing shareholders. This means that the shareholders will be able to subscribe to the new shares at a price that is lower than the current market price.

It's not a good practice to subscribe to all the rights issue; do your research before subscribing. Sometimes, the rights issue price will be similar the current market price; in such a case, it's better to not subscribe.

Usually the allocation will be in terms of ratio such as 1:5, 1:10 etc.

Example

Assume Company X announces 1:5 rights issue; this means that for every five shares you hold you can subscribe to one additional share.

Buyback of shares

Shareholder shares are bought back at a fixed price through a buyback. This happens when a company has excess cash and desires to reduce the number of shares in the open market. Usually, buyback prices are slightly higher than current market prices in order to reward existing shareholders. After the buyback, the liquidity of shares decreases and stock price increases.

Companies announce buyback for the following reasons:

A. To lure new investors
B. When a company feels that its stock is undervalued they announce buy backs to increase the value of their share.

C. To increase the promoter holding percentage.
D. To give confidence to the shareholders.
E. To avoid threats from shareholders who are interested in controlling stake.
F. To delist the company at a later stage.
G. Instead of paying dividends, some companies offer the buyback option as an incentive to reward share holders.

Dividends

Dividends are a portion of the profit given by the company to its shareholders; they are usually a percentage of the face value of the stock.

Dividends received from foreign companies are taxable, whereas dividend received from domestic companies - up to 10,00,000 per annum - is tax-free. If the aggregate dividend received from a domestic company during the year exceeds Rs 10,00,000, then a tax rate of ten percent is applicable.

For example, say Mr. Kumar receives a dividend of Rs 12 lakh form different Indian companies during the year. Since his dividend income exceeds Rs 10 lakh, he has to pay tax at ten percent on dividend income in excess of Rs 10 lakh. Hence, the tax payable will be Rs 20,000 (10% on 2 lakhs)

Some companies don't give dividends and some give one or more dividends per year. Remember, it is possible for a loss making company to give dividends from excess cash reserves.

Companies that don't pay dividends are not bad. It just means that they have decided to reinvest the profits back into the business instead of paying shareholders the profits.

Example

If a stock's face value is Rs. 10 and the company announces a dividend of fifty percent, you will get Rs.5 as dividend for each stock you hold.

Rs.10 * 50% = 10*(50/100) = Rs.5

When exactly should one buy to get the benefits?

The following are the four important dates related to any corporate action.

- Dividend Declaration Date
- Ex Dividend Date
- Record Date
- Dividend Payout Date

If you are planning to buy a stock for dividend, make sure you buy the stock before the Ex Dividend Date. On Ex Dividend Date the stock price quotes at minus the dividend per share. Let me explain this with an example:

Sun	Mon	Tues	Wed	Thu	Fri	Sat
	1	2	3	4	5	6
7	8	9	10	11	12	13
14	15	16	17	18	19	20
21	22	23	24	25	26	27
28	29	30				

3rd	4th to 16th	17th	19th	26th
Dividend Declaration Date	Buy shares during this period to enjoy dividend	Ex dividend date	Record date	Payout date

Company X calls the Board of Directors for an Annual General Meeting (AGM) to decide about dividends on the 3rd - this date is called the Dividend Declaration Date. If the company's board approves the dividend issue, they decide the Record Date (19th).

The Record Date (19th) is the date on which the company freezes the list of shareholders who are eligible for dividend. There is usually ample time between the Dividend Declaration Date and Record Date that gives investors enough time to buy stocks for dividends.

The Ex Dividend Date (17th) is always two days before the Record Date (19th). In India, stock settlement is T+2 days; this means that the stocks will be deposited in your demat account after two working days.

If you are buying a stock for dividend, make sure you buy it before the ex dividend date (17th), because settlement takes two working days; only then will your name appear in the company's register on the Record Date.

Remember, on Ex Dividend date the stock price quotes at minus the dividend per share; i.e., if the share price is Rs.50 on the day before Ex Dividend Date and the company has declared Rs.5 as dividend per share, on ex dividend date, the price will be adjusted by Rs.5 and the share will be available at Rs.45.

Dividend Payout Date (26th) is the date on which the company pays dividend to its shareholders. This will happen at least a week or two after the record date (19th).

Nifty BeES

Nifty BeES is an ETF (Exchange Traded Fund) by Goldman Sachs, which trades on the National Stock Exchange. Each Nifty BeES unit is 1/10th of the Nifty Index value. Nifty BeES units are traded and settled in dematerialised form - like any other stock in the open market. The performance of Nifty BeES is simply the result of performance of all the shares in the Nifty Index.

Investing in Nifty BeES is very simple carries lesser risk, because one unit gives exposure to fifty shares of the Nifty Index and risks are spread over a single entity. The value of Nifty BeES would appreciate if Nifty increases and it would fall if Nifty decreases.

Non-performing companies are replaced by performing companies; hence your investment is always protected. The Exchange trade funds have computer programs to do this automatically. A few years ago, when Satyam Computers were in trouble the stock exchange replaced it with Sun Pharmaceutical - the country's largest drug maker.

Don't buy all the fifty companies in the Nifty Index individually. Because, by buying Nifty BeES, a small amount is enough to buy a portion of all the fifty stocks; but, a large investment is required to buy one single share of all Nifty companies. Moreover, managing the portfolio and fund allocation for all fifty companies is time consuming; added to this, reshuffling the portfolio whenever a company is removed from the index is a headache.

If you are a beginner and don't know where to start, follow the strategy below.

Buy N shares of Nifty BeES every month.

Example

From your savings take twenty five percent and invest in Nifty BeES every month irrespective of whether the market goes up or down.

If you have monthly savings of Rs.20,000, then invest Rs.5,000 on a monthly basis in Nifty BeES; by investing every month, you will have a few hundred shares in five years; in doing so, you have wisely invested in fifty stocks spread over about twenty two sectors - at one shot.

It is definitely less risky than buying a separate company's stocks. Even if one particular sector were not to perform well, there would be other sectors that will compensate; therefore, you can be at peace and your investment will grow even if a few sectors underperform; this guarantees a fifteen percent annual return over a period of ten years.

Advantages of Nifty BeES

1. Unlike Mutual Funds, Nifty BeES is a no load scheme.
2. Nifty BeES is liquid and is readily available in the open market.
3. Nifty BeES is neutral because there is no fund manager bias.

4. Investing in a single unit gives you an exposure to fifty shares of the Nifty index- easy and instant diversification.
5. You will get dividend for Nifty BeES.

Various criteria for a stock to be included in the index:

- **Domicile**: The company must be domiciled in India and trade on the NSE.
- **Market capitalization**: The company's most recent six-month average market capitalization should be Rs.500 crores or more.
- **Free float**: Investable Weight Factor (IWF) must be at least ten percent. It includes details about a company's shares that are readily available for trading. This doesn't include shares held by the company's promoters.
- **Liquidity**: For inclusion in the index, the security should have traded at an average impact cost of 0.50 % or less during the last six months for 90% of the observations for a portfolio of Rs. 10 crores.
- **Listing criteria**: A company should have a minimum listing history of six months for inclusion. A company that comes out with an IPO is eligible for inclusion in the index if it fulfills the normal eligibility criteria for the

index - impact cost and float-adjusted market capitalization for a three-month period.
- **Differential Voting Rights:** Equity securities with Differential Voting Rights (DVR) are eligible for inclusion.
- **F&O criteria for stocks in NIFTY 50:** In order to become eligible for inclusion in NIFTY 50, a stock must be available for trading in NSE's Futures & Options segment.
- **Trading Frequency:** The stock should have been traded on each and every trading day in the last three months.

Different types of BeES

There are many exchange trade funds. Some of them are mentioned below.

1. Bank BeES
The Bank BeES is Goldman Sachs Bank ETF fund; it holds all of the Bank Nifty Twelve stocks. Any investor who wants to invest in the top banks of the Indian economy can do so by investing in the Bank BeES. A performing bank will replace a non-performing bank making sure your investment is always protected.

2. Gold BeES
Gold ETFs are open-ended mutual fund schemes that allow investment in gold in small denominations, which makes it easier for the retail investor to participate.

They provide returns that would track the returns from physical gold in the spot market very closely. The minimum lot is one unit and these units can be redeemed either directly from the fund or from the market.

3. Reliance Liquid BeES

Liquid BeES is an open ended liquid scheme with daily dividend and compulsory reinvestment of dividend. Liquid BeES can be bought directly from NSE. One unit of liquid BeES costs Rs.1000; liquid BeES always cost Rs.1000. Are you wondering how it is possible to earn if the price remains constant? It is possible, because the returns are in the form of dividend and not by capital appreciation.

Sometimes investors will not have any viable investment options and the money in their trading accounts sit idle without earning interest. During these times an investor can buy liquid BeES and earn dividend. Whenever a buying opportunity arises investors can easily sell the liquid BeES (highly liquid) and pay their margin money. The good news is that dividend earned through liquid BeES is tax-free.

The quarterly result of a company - what to see & what to ignore?

Consider the following while analyzing a company's quarterly results:

1. Evaluate whether the changes in sales, expenses and profitability are because of short-term factors or long-term structural changes. Never confuse a short-term change for a long-term trend change.
2. Check the "notes to accounts" section for explanations and updates on key business aspects.
3. For cyclical companies, businesses are seasonal in nature. Hence, wide variations in performance from quarter to quarter must be seen in the correct context.
4. In addition to the quarterly profit & loss statement, companies publish their balance sheets bi-annually. Check for significant changes therein on a year-on-year basis.
5. Some companies publish presentations along with their quarterly results and even participate in conference calls and analyst meets to discuss quarterly performance and future prospects.

Global economic factors that can affect your portfolio

In a globalised world, a change happening in one part of the world can have far-reaching effects in any part of the world.

There are two major global economic events:

1. Changes in Liquidity
2. Changes in Earnings

Changes in Liquidity

Change in liquidity changes the direction in which money flows in the financial system. These changes in money flows are a short-term event and not driven by fundamentals. Such money flows either inflate stock price or deflate them, albeit temporarily.

A hike in interest rates by the US Fed can partially reverse the money flow back into the US financial system; this can cause stock prices to come down.

In contrast, take the US Federal Reserve's quantitative easing program - this is nothing but an unprecedented money printing exercise by the US central bank. A lot of this 'easy money' can come to emerging markets like India. This kind of excess liquidity can cause stock prices to rise.

Change in Earnings

Change in earnings occurs due to change in demand and supply of labor.

For example, when Chinese labor becomes expensive because of rapid increase in wages, export-oriented sectors like India tend to be benefitted as India has lower labor costs compared to China.

On the other hand, currency exchange rates affect travel, exports, imports and the economy. When the Chinese Yuan depreciates against rupee; it adversely impacts the business of Indian exporters. To put it simply - a cheaper Yuan could result in more imports from China.

Stock screener

There are more than 5000 stocks listed on the stock exchange. It is humanly impossible to look into the financials of all the listed companies. Stock screeners help us eliminate stocks that don't fit the prerequisite financial criteria. Stock screening doesn't help a trader predict the direction in which the stocks are going to move; instead, it helps an investor to identify good quality stocks. Through stock screeners one can compare a stock with its peers and take wise buy/sell decisions. Some investors prefer fundamental screener; others prefer technical screener; while the rest prefer using a combination of both to filter out better stocks.

Limitations of stock screeners

Stock screeners are great stock picking tools, but they too have their limitations.

1. They only indicate a company's past performance and don't provide any information about the company's future prospects.
2. Investors should not trust the results provided by a stock screener blindly. That information should be used as a starting point for further research after which investment decisions should be made.
3. Stock screener is a statistical tool, so the quality factor of stocks is not taken into account.

Various filters used in stock screeners

A person can screen stocks based on many criteria. Some of them are listed below:

1. Most undervalued p/e.
2. Most undervalued p/b.
3. Fastest growing companies by profits.
4. Best dividend yield stocks.
5. Banks and financial institutions with best asset quality.
6. Companies with highest shareholder return.

What is alpha and beta of a stock and why is it important?

Alpha

Alpha is used to measure the performance on a risk-adjusted basis. Its purpose is to know if an investor is being compensated for the volatility risk taken. Simply put, Alpha is a measure of risk.

Usually Alpha is a number assigned to the return over a given index. So if you invest in a stock and it returns twenty percent while the Nifty earned five percent, then you have an Alpha of fifteen.

A positive alpha of 1.0 means the fund or stock has outperformed its benchmark index by one percent. A similar negative alpha of 1.0 would indicate an underperformance of one percent.

Alpha greater than zero means an investment outperformed.

A negative Alpha means that the investment underperformed.

Beta

Beta is a historical measure of relative volatility. Beta measures how volatile an investment is compared to the overall market. A beta of 1.0 indicates that the investment will move with the market; a beta of less than 1.0 means that the investment will be less volatile than the market - it means the stock price does not fluctuate as much.

Example

- If the Beta is -2 then the stock moves in the opposite direction from the index by a factor of two.
- If a stock's beta is 1.4, then theoretically it's 40% more volatile than the market.

Conclusion

Both Alpha and Beta are backwards looking risk ratios - all calculations are made using past data. Remember, past performance is no guarantee of future results. Alpha and Beta can only help to differentiate between relatively good and relatively poor investments over a given period of time.

Key parameters to keep in mind while analyzing various sectors

The analysis pattern differs for each and every sector and we take a look at them below.

FMCG

Key financials and valuation ratios to look at while analyzing an FMCG sector.

- ROCE (Return On Capital Employed) trend. It will give you an idea of how effectively the company is optimizing its resources.
- Dividend paying track record for the past five years.
- Look at the P/E (price to earnings ratio), market capitalization to sales and profit before tax.
- CAGR for the past five years. Real growth is because of successful new product introduction and growth in market share.
- Operating margin – look at whether the trend is improving or declining. It will improve if there is an efficient supply chain and it will decline if advertising spends have increased due to intense competition.
- Cash flows and the working capital efficiency will give you an idea of the company's bargaining power as well as its ability to utilize its resources.

Banking

Price to book value (P/BV) is very important while analyzing banking stocks. Since cash is the raw material for any bank, the ability to grow in the long-term, therefore, depends on the capital in the bank, where capital is the net worth. To get a real picture of the available capital, remember to deduct the overall non-performing asset from the net worth.

Investors need to double-check the quality of management before investing.

Cement

Following are the key aspects and valuation ratios to look at while analyzing the cement sector:

Apart from the P/E ratio, one also has to look at the PCF ratio (Price to Cash flow). As the cement industry is capital intensive, depreciation is huge and has to be taken into account.

- **Geographical presence** - The company should not have all its plants concentrated in one region. It should have a geographical spread so that adverse market conditions in one region can be mitigated by high growth in another.
- **Power** - Power costs form the most critical cost component in cement manufacturing - about twenty five to thirty percent of total expenses.

Companies having captive power plants can reduce power costs and get uninterrupted supply of power.
- **Freight** - Cement is a heavy commodity and transporting it is a costly affair - about twelve to fifteen percent of total expenses. Companies that have plants located in coastal belts find that it is cheaper to transport cement via the sea route to cater to coastal markets such as Mumbai, Gujarat and Tamil Nadu.

Software

Following are the key things to look at before investing in a software stock:

- **Management future vision** - The management's ability to foresee threats/opportunities without diverting from the vision is important. The companies' annual reports and their official web site give a snapshot of the management's future vision.
- **Employee productivity** - Productivity = revenue per employee divided by cost per employee. Comparing this ratio with the peer group gives a better clarity for taking investment decisions.
- **Financial ratios** - P/E, Return on Equity, Return on Assets and Return on Capital and Operating margins have to be considered.

Telecom

Key financial metrics - It is important to look at these ratios for the past three years:

- Average revenue per user
- Subscriber growth
- Profit Before Interest and Tax/Interest (PBIT)
- Earnings Per Share (EPS)
- Debt to Equity Ratio
- Return on Equity (ROE)
- Return on Capital Employed (ROCE)
- Free cash flow = [Profit after tax + Depreciation - Dividend & Dividend Tax - Capex -Working capital changes]
- Enterprise value per subscriber ratio indicates the price at which a company can be bought over.
- Price to cash flow (P/CF)
- P/E

Construction

Key things to look at before investing in the construction sector:

- Order-book to sales ratio
- Working capital to sales
- Debt to equity
- Return On Capital Employed
- Price to Earnings (P/E) ratio
- Price to Sales ratio (P/S) ratio

Pharmaceutical

Key things to look at before investing in the pharmaceutical sector:

- R&D expenditure as a percentage of revenues.
- Government policies have a major influence on the domestic pharmaceutical sector
- Good Management - hiring 'the right person at the right place' is key to the success of any company - annual reports contain all this information.
- P/E ratio.

Scam

Listed below are the two most common scams in the Indian stock market.

Scam 1 - Buy/Sell Tips Fraud

This is the most common scam in the Indian stock market. Usually, fraudsters advertise in all possible ways to lure traders and investors; they promise forty to fifty percent return per month with a ninety percent accuracy rate. They provide free tips for a period of three days to trap unsuspecting people. Everything is set up such that all the tips provided by them during the trial period will be 100% accurate. The convincing results lead people to subscribe to their highly priced monthly/quarterly/yearly subscriptions. Sadly, none of their tips work after subscribing.

You may wonder how these fraudsters are able to provide 100% accurate tips during the trial period alone.

Usually fraudsters offer a three-day trial period. They give only one recommendation to buy/sell a stock on all three days.

These tips are not sent to an individual; instead, a group of 1000 people or more receive these tips. They procure access to such a large number of contacts (name, mobile phone numbers, email IDs) through agencies that sell them this data. Exercise caution when you share your personal information in shopping malls, theatres, lucky draws or any other kind of promotional activities, because your personal information is sold to such fraudsters in the form of a database.

Now, let's see what happens every day during the trial period.

Day1 - They divide the group into two. Let's say group A contains 500 and group B contains 500 people. They send an SMS to group A asking them to sell a particular stock (usually a volatile well known stock) when the market opens; they ask group B to buy the same stock at market opening. Obviously, either the stock will go up or down after a few hours. After some time they will ask to book profit / loss. Therefore, on day one, they have sent a successful tip to 500 people. They, discard the other 500 people who booked loss.

Day2 - They again divide the 500 successful people into two groups. Now they send an SMS to 250 people asking them to sell a particular volatile stock and the remaining 250 to buy the same stock at market opening. Again, one group will receive correct recommendation and they discard the other group which booked loss.

Day3 - They again divide the successful 250 people into two groups. And they send 'buy' tips of a particular company to 125 people and 'sell' tips for the same company to the remaining 125 people. Finally, 125 people will receive a correct tip for three consecutive days and these 125 people are trapped since they have been tricked into thinking that the recommendations are 100% accurate. Most of them subscribe to the monthly/quarterly/annual recommendation plan and become a victim of the scam. Assuming the annual subscription plan costs Rs.20,000, even if 50 out of 125 people subscribe, these fraudsters will get Rs 10 lakhs.

Once they subscribe, the tips will not work like they earlier did and they will lose their subscription money. In addition to that they will end up in loss by trading based on incorrect tips.

Scam 2 - Penny stock fraud

In micro cap stock/penny stock fraud, the fraudsters try to boost the price of the micro cap stocks by providing fake information to traders. Fraudsters follow the below mentioned steps to fool greedy people.

- First, they buy a cheap micro cap stock in large quantity.
- Then they send false information to many traders recommending them to buy that particular stock. For example, the micro cap has won a case and is going to get a huge sum of money as compensation or a big company is taking over that penny stock; or the micro cap stock is giving a bonus of 1:1; or a blue chip is buying huge stake of that micro cap stock.
- Those who are greedy and those who want to make quick money start buying these micro cap stocks.
- As the demand increases, the price of that stock starts moving up.
- Once the share price reaches a fair price, then these fraudsters sell their holdings and make good money.
- Once the fraudsters sell their holding at high prices, they stop sending fake news. As the demand decreases the price of these stocks come down and the greedy traders holding position in that company lose their money.

Scam summary

1. Don't buy shares recommended over phone.
2. Be skeptical about "double your money instantly" ads.
3. Don't invest in any software for buy/sell analysis.
4. Don't buy penny shares.

How to choose a stock advisor?

There are two kinds of advisors:

1. Fee based Advisor
2. Commission based Advisor

Fee based Advisor

A fee-based advisor collects a flat fee for investment advice. This works like a subscription model for a defined period - one month/ six months / twelve months/ lifetime. They provide buy/sell calls for short-term trading and good IPO suggestions among others.

Advantages of a fee based advisor

- No bias on investment recommendations.
- Greater transparency.
- Potential tax benefits.

Commission based Advisor

Commission based advisors collect a commission for every buy and sell calls. Whether the client earns or not, for every transaction a small commission is paid to the advisor. They give many intraday tips on a daily basis and they prefer traders to investors, because trader's trade often and they get regular commissions.

Conclusion

A fee-based advisor is always better than a commission based advisor because the sole intention of the fee based advisor is to generate good returns out of your investments; whereas, the intention of commission based advisors is to make you trade more and guarantee their commission.

Why not mutual funds?

All mutual fund houses charge for managing the funds - fund managers salary, distribution costs etc. Depending on the fund, these charges can be significant. When you exit from your mutual fund, you might be charged an extra cost as exit load (an exit load is applicable if you sell your investments within a specified duration).

Moreover, in mutual funds, major gains get diluted. Diversification has an averaging effect on your investments. While diversification saves you from suffering any major losses, it also prevents you from making any major gains.

The below table gives a detailed picture of the liberties enjoyed by any individual investor vs. fund manager

Individual Investor	**Mutual Fund Manager**
He can invest in any small cap stock	He cannot invest in small cap stocks
He can hold the stock for as many years he wishes.	He cannot hold the stock for a very long period.
He can even invest thirty percent or more of the total portfolio in a single quality stock. No one can dictate terms.	Mutual funds usually have restrictions pertaining to investing large percentages of money in a single quality stock.

Conclusion

Say no to mutual fund if:

- You have enough time to research quality stocks.
- You have your own trustable fee based equity advisor.

Stocks to avoid when it comes to investment

- High debt companies with debt to equity ratio of more than 1.
- Companies with low promoter holding.
- Micro caps.
- High promoter pledging. Avoid if more than thirty percent of promoter holdings are pledged.
- Stocks touching new low.
- Companies that encourage costly acquisition.

What one should do during a market crash?

a. During a market crash concentrate on the shares that haven't fallen.
b. Buy the quality stocks at a fair price when everyone is panic selling.
c. Check your portfolio for any non-performers and use this as an opportunity to replace them with high quality stocks.
d. Never chase or bet on past performers - e.g.: Satyam Computers, Suzlon.
e. The first thing you do when in need of cash is to sell all the non-performers in your portfolio. But, people usually do the opposite - they sell all the good stocks for a little profit; after a few months, the good stocks they sold will go up and the bad stocks that they held on to will come down further.

Common mistakes investors make

1. Holding bad quality stocks / losers for a very long time hoping that they will bounce back to the bought price.
2. Selling high quality stocks / winners too early.
3. If a stock is at fifty-two weeks low, don't buy that stock blindly. Do your research before buying. If the business is not strong there are chances that the stock price will touch new fifty-two weeks low every day. Eg: Kingfisher Airlines.
4. Don't hesitate to buy a stock that has touched fifty-two weeks high. There may be more room for the stock to climb. Eg. MRF Tyres

Ask yourself the following questions before investing in a stock:

- What is the market capitalization of the company?
- What are the annual pretax profits?
- Are profits rising yoy (year on year)?
- What is the net debt?
- Is the debt equity ratio < 1?
- Is debt under three times the annual profits?
- Is it a cyclical or non-cyclical company?
- Is ROCE improving yoy?
- Is RONW improving yoy?
- Is it liquid?
- Is the sector doing well?
- Is the demand for product/service likely to grow?

All the above details can be obtained from the link below.

www.moneycontrol.com

Factors to be considered before investing in a company

1. As much as possible choose a non-cyclical company.
2. If u can't understand the company's business, don't invest.
3. Look into the market capitalization of the company. Don't invest in a company that has a market capital of less than Rs. 500 crores.
4. Study the profit/loss statement of the past three years. Invest only if the market capitalization is within the range of twenty times the annual profit before tax.
5. Invest only if the debt to equity ratio is less than 1.
6. Compare the sector p.e with the stock p.e.
7. Check for three years history of dividend or bonus.
8. ROCE (Return On Capital Employed) & RONW (Return On Net Worth) must be more than twelve percent per annum.
9. Revenue growth should be at least ten percent year on year.

Misconceptions

Don't fall prey to the following misconceptions:

- Low price stocks are cheap and high price stocks are expensive.
- Investing in low PE stocks is called value investing.
- Stocks at fifty-two weeks high are not safe.
- Stocks at fifty-two weeks low can go up.
- Previous bull market stocks are a good investment bet.
- Stocks that fall sharply have to move up sharply.

Dos & Don'ts

Dos:

1. Allocate at least half an hour a day to educate yourself on market news and ways to manage your portfolio.
2. Follow at least two web sites or magazines for market and company news.
3. Allocate fifty percent of your savings every month for the share market. For example, if you earn Rs.1,00,000 / month, and your savings are Rs.40,000, then you can allocate Rs. 20,000 for the share market.
4. Build your equity portfolio gradually.

Don'ts:

1. Avoid trading over phone. Learn to place your orders online. Preferably ask your broker to give you a demo.
2. Don't blindly follow the tips given by your stockbroker or any analyst, for that matter. Do thorough research before buying/selling.
3. Don't invest using borrowed capital.

Final words

Dear Investors, if you want to reap maximum benefits from your investments remember the following:

- Do not follow daily price movements of the stocks that you have invested in; instead follow company specific announcements and news.
- Do not follow any tips, news or analysts blindly. Thoroughly check all the parameters we have discussed in this chapter before taking any investment decisions.
- Do not worry about market corrections or market crashes - they are temporary; instead, use this opportunity to buy quality stocks.
- Do not panic sell.

CHAPTER 3

Secrets for Smart Traders

There are two types of traders:

- Intraday traders
- Short term trader / Smart trader

Intraday trader

An intraday trader opens and closes a position in a security on the same trading day. Intraday traders usually have very little capital or they trade with borrowed money. They trade during the entire market hours and try to enter and close as many trades as possible.

As the brokerage charged for intraday is very less, intraday traders buy and sell for a meager profit. Stockbrokers love them, because they spend the entire day trading as much as possible and making the stockbroker rich.

Most intraday traders use shorter duration time frame charts [1M, 5M, 15M (M-minute)] to decide their entry and exit points; these time frame charts are not accurate and cannot be trusted blindly.

Why is the term "Stop loss" famous with intraday traders?

Intraday traders generally trade with stop loss. The actual purpose of this is to restrict loss to a certain extent.

In reality, the intraday traders unknowingly place stop loss to generate loss. The following example will explain this in detail.

Example:

An intraday trader buys a share at Rs. 100 and sets a stop-loss at Rs. 98. He is planning to sell if the stock price touches Rs. 103 on the same day. But there's no way he or she can predict the direction of price movement accurately for smaller time frames in a fluctuating market. There is nothing to protect from a situation where the stock price comes down to Rs. 98 first and then bounces back to Rs.103. In this case, the stop-loss gets executed first -- the stock sells at Rs.98, and the intraday trader misses the opportunity to sell at Rs.103 and ends up in loss.

Sorry to say this, but the sure-shot way to lose money in the stock market is by doing intraday trading.

If you are an intraday trader ask yourself the following questions:

- By the end of every financial year, did you see a net profit or loss doing intraday trades?
- Is the time spent sitting in front of the computer doing intraday worth the money you have earned?
- Who earned more in every trade? You or your stock broker?
- Did you have peace of mind doing intraday trading?

Be true to yourself and write the answers next to each and every question. This exercise will give you a clear picture of how you have traded all these days in the stock market.

Dear reader's acceptance is the first step to self-development. The problem with many people is that, they know what they do is wrong, but they don't want to accept it, which restricts development.

How people fall prey to intraday trading?

- Many stock brokers give free tips to do intraday, tempting clients to buy or sell. Whether or

not you make a profit, the broker gets his commission for your buy and sell order.
- People with less capital do intraday. Because they don't have enough money to take delivery.
- Stock brokers attract clients by offering different brokerage slabs based on the volume they do. To put it simply the brokerage percentage is much lower when you do huge volumes. Most traders don't realize that by doing too many trades, only the brokerage gets cheaper and your chance of earning never increases.
- People with lots of time tend to be intraday traders. They follow the market all day just to kill time, and eventually lose their capital.

Don'ts:

- Don't trade daily. Wait for concrete opportunity.
- Don't follow any analyst's tips blindly.
- Don't do intraday, based on buy/sell signals generated from charting software with lesser time frame.
- Don't waste your hard earned money by subscribing to intraday tips.

Remember by doing intraday trading only your stock broker becomes rich.

The only way to make more money in the stock market is by doing less. Most intraday traders have a gambling mentality and want to make quick money. Remember, what comes quick will go quick. There is no shortcut to wealth creation.

"Stop doing intraday to start earning."

Common mistakes that intraday traders make:

- Short selling in equity is similar to forced intraday trading. If you don't buy and cover your position, the broker will automatically square off the position at the end of the market operating time.
- Nowadays, intra-day traders have begun investing in automated systems for trading. They simply switch the programs on and let the computer do the rest of the work. But, this automation rarely works leading to huge losses and, if lucky, very negligible profits.

However, if you're still interested in intraday trading, pick a stock based on the following criteria:

- Look for stocks with high liquidity and moderate volatility.
- Trade strong stocks (long buy and sell) in an uptrend and weak stocks (short sell and buy) in the downtrend.

- When the market is sideways or range-bound (moves within a relatively tight price range), don't trade.
- If there is any hot news about a particular sector or stock, choose that sector or stock to trade for the day.

Conclusion

If there is anything good about intraday trading it is that it starts afresh each day and were you in a position of profit the previous day, nothing can happen overnight to ruin it.

Intraday traders are at the top of the risk spectrum because intraday trading is like gambling. I urge my readers to not indulge in intraday trading with borrowed money.

Short-term trader

A short-term trader opens and closes a position in a security within a maximum period of twelve months. They are known to be very patient while entering a trade and extremely aggressive when getting out. Short-term traders trade only when there is an opportunity.

They trade based on the following:

1. Chart based trading
2. News based trading

Chart Based Trading

Chart based traders rely only on higher time frame charts and not news about the company; the charts are used to decided the entry and exit points.

Charts can be analyzed in the following time frames:

Monthly Charts - every candlestick represents a month. Monthly charts are most often only used by long-term investors and not by others. As a rule of thumb, these charts are commonly used to analyze time periods in excess of two years.

Weekly Charts - every candlestick represents a week. Traders and investors, whose time-horizon is longer, use weekly charts. As a rule of thumb, weekly charts are commonly used to analyze periods in excess of six months.

Daily Charts - every candlestick represents a day. Daily charts are, perhaps, the most commonly used charts by traders and investors. As a rule of thumb, daily charts are commonly used to analyze periods in excess of six weeks.

Hourly chart - every candlestick represents an hour. Hourly charts are commonly used for swing or short-term types of trades that last from a few hours to several days.

Minutes chart - every candlestick represents a minute. Minute charts are commonly used for day trades, especially to decide entry and exit points.

News based trading

News-based traders are on the look out for news that involve change in management, rumors about mergers and corporate actions (such as buybacks and change in interest rates). Given that these are all events that can cause a company's share price to rise or fall, they are of utmost importance to the news-based trader. Economic news spurts strong short-term moves in the markets, thereby creating trading opportunities.

Derivatives

When you buy stock, you own a part of the company and are eligible for bonus or dividend - if declared. In case of derivatives, however, none of these benefits are available; you don't even need a demat account for trading derivatives, because all derivative transactions are settled with cash. Contract positions are held with the exchange until they expire. You will need just a trading and savings account to trade derivatives.

The two types of derivatives available in the Indian stock market are:

1. Futures
2. Options

Futures

Futures create an opportunity to trade more with little cash. The trader has to pay only a margin amount to buy/sell the index/stock futures. If the price moves in the trader's favor, during the course of the contract, the trader makes profit or else he incurs losses.

Not all the companies listed in the stock exchange offer futures contracts; companies whose shares have high liquidity and volume are eligible for futures trading.

For a futures contract worth Rs 6 lakhs, one pays only ten to fifteen percent margin money to broker - which is Rs 60,000 – Rs. 90,000. Margin percentage differs from stock to stock based on the risks involved; which further depends on the liquidity and volatility of the respective shares; along with the general market conditions. Normally index futures have lesser margin than the stock futures because they are comparatively less volatile in nature.

Unlike stocks, derivatives have an expiry date - the last Thursday of every month. If that day turns out to be a holiday, then contracts expire on the previous trading day.

Margin money is calculated every day based on the closing price of the stock. Settlements are done on a daily basis (MTM-Mark to Market) until the contract expires. Profits and losses are calculated (and credited/

debited in traders' account) at the end of every day. This means that the profits or losses are calculated based on the difference between the previous day and the current day's settlement price. If the trader doesn't have enough margin money the broker can sell his F&O contract and recover the money.

Consider that you are buying one lot of NIFTY Futures (50 shares)

If the previous day's closing Price = Rs 9900

And today's closing price = Rs 9960

Then, net profit = (9960-9900)*50 = Rs 3000

The same process of MTM (Mark to Market) is repeated and profit/losses are calculated every day until the position is closed or it expires. Though the profit/loss is credited/debited on daily basis in traders account, the brokerages/fees/taxes are only charged at the time of buying and selling future contract.

Advantages of Futures

1. The charges for the commission on futures trading are relatively small when compared to other type of investments.
2. Futures contracts are highly leveraged financial instruments that permit achieving greater gains using a limited amount of invested funds.

Disadvantages of Futures

1. Leverage can make trading in futures contracts highly risky.
2. It offers only a partial hedge.

Things to remember while trading stock futures:

1. It easier to pick a bad stock from a bad sector in a bear market than to identify a good stock to trade, in the bull market. Moreover the fall is deeper and quicker than the rise. It's wiser to wait for a market crash or bad news about a particular sector and make use of that opportunity to short a poorly performing stock (sell and buy).
2. Don't be greedy and never trade with a gamblers mentality.
3. Trade with only one lot at a time even if you have money for three lots, because you will need money for MTM(Mark to Market) and for averaging.
4. Don't lose more than two percent of your capital in a single trade. Cultivate that discipline.

Position Trading Technique

There are many techniques for chart based trading, but I prefer stock maximiser technique. Instead of learning all the techniques just master one technique and use it wisely.

This technique is applicable only for position trading not for intraday trading.

Closely monitor the price movement of one or two stocks and use charts (the stock maximiser technique) to make decide when to enter and when to exit.

Before going in depth, one needs to know the following terms to understand the stock maximiser technique.

Candlestick

A candlestick displays the high, low, opening and closing prices of a security for a specific period of time.

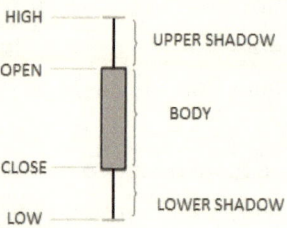

Moving average

Moving Average (MA) is an indicator of whether a trend is following or lagging, because it is based on past prices and it filters out the 'noise' from random price fluctuations. MA is is calculated by adding the closing price of the security for a number of time periods and then dividing this total by the number of time periods.

Generally, traders prefer the twenty-day or fifty-day moving average.

Parabolic SAR

Parabolic SAR is used by traders to determine the direction of the movement of price and also the point at which it switches direction; it is also known as the stop and reversal system.

It is shown as a series of dots placed either above or below a candle on a chart.

ADX

The Average Directional Index (ADX) is an indicator used to quantify trend strength. Remember, ADX is non-directional and only indicates trend strength. ADX is plotted as a single line, with values ranging from a low of zero to a high of 100. Generally, traders use ADX readings above sixteen to confirm that the trend is strong. Conversely, when ADX is below sixteen, trading is avoided.

MACD

Moving Average Convergence/Divergence (MACD) shows the duration of a trend in a stock's price.

We will not be getting into the details as learning the basics is enough. Software like Chart Nexus allows us to easily pick and choose the required indicators.

Stock maximiser technique

First choose the stock you want to trade in; add the four above-mentioned indicators in a day chart and a weekly chart; follow the below-mentioned steps for buying and selling.

First, look at the day chart and then look at the weekly chart; if both the charts suggest the same, then trade; else, choose a different stock or wait for a better trading opportunity.

Case 1 - For Long/ Uptrend

To buy:

1. The stock is in uptrend and goes above the twenty-day or fifty-day moving average (MA).
2. MA is in an uptrend.
3. Parabolic SAR is below price.

4. Preferably MACD crossover at the bottom.
5. Preferably ADX > 16

To sell/exit:

1. When Parabolic SAR is above price.
2. MACD crossover is at the top - whichever comes first.

Case 2 - For short/ downtrend

To sell:

1. The stock is in downtrend and goes below the twenty-day or fifty-day moving average (MA).
2. MA is in downtrend.
3. Parabolic SAR is above price.
4. Preferably MACD crossover at the top
5. Preferably ADX > 16

To buy/exit:

1. When Parabolic SAR is below price.
2. MACD crossover is at the bottom - whichever comes first.

Standard & Poor's 500 Index - S&P 500 futures

The Standard & Poor's 500 Index (S&P 500) is an index containing 500 large companies with huge market capitalization. It is seen as a leading indicator of U.S. equities and a reflection of the performance of the large-cap universe. The S&P 500 is regarded as the most accurate gauge of the performance of large-cap American equities. The companies included in the S&P 500 list are selected by: the S&P Index Committee, a team of analysts and economists at Standard & Poor's.

The National Stock Exchange (NSE) has launched derivatives based on S&P and Dow Jones indices since 29 August 2011. Many traders are not aware of this S&P futures contract. The contract size is 250 units and, usually, the expiry date is the third Friday of the contract month; in case third Friday is a holiday in USA or in India, the contract shall expire on the preceding business day. Last half hour's weighted average price is the daily settlement price and the settlement is done in INR.

Things to remember while trading S&P futures:

1. Never short; always go for long (buy and then sell); because, if you see the S&P 500 graph for the past ten years, you will notice that the

price has gradually increased and that there is no sharp decline.
2. S&P 500 trades twenty-four hours a day in the US market, but, as Indians, we can only place orders during NSE market hours.
3. If you are new to F&O, practice paper trade with S&P futures.
4. Wait for the opportunity and trade S&P futures only during Bull Run.
5. Don't be greedy, because when the Indian market is closed the S&P 500 can still move and could come down; you could be in for a shock when the Indian market opens the next day.

Benefits of trading the S&P futures:

- You would be able to speculate directly in the top US equity indices.
- Trading would be in Indian rupees, so there is no foreign exchange risk.
- Trading would be during Indian trading hours.
- Opportunity for you to diversify based on geography.
- There is no upper limit on investment since these derivative contracts are denominated in Indian rupees.

Options

An option is a derivative and its value is based on the underlying stock (equity) or underlying index.

If an option is exercisable on or before the expiry date it is called an American option; and if it is exercisable only on expiry date it is called a European option. In India we only deal with European options.

There are two kinds of options - Call Options and Put Options.

Call Options

A Call Option is an option to buy a stock at a specific price on or before a certain date. Call options are like security deposits; for example, if you want to pre-book a hotel room, you are asked for a security deposit. This money is then used as an advance and the hotelier will block a room for the said dates; if you don't show up on that date, you will not get your security deposit back, but will have no other liability.

Similarly, when you buy a Call Option, the price you pay for it is called the option premium; this secures your right to buy a certain stock at a specified price called the strike price; if you decide not to use the option to buy the stock, your only expense would have been the option premium.

Put options

Put Options help sell a stock at a specific price on or before a certain date; they are like insurance policies. For example, when you buy a new car, you pay a premium and get insurance; if damage occurs to the car, you can use your policy to get the insured value of the car. If the car remains damage-free, then the insurance is redundant and the insurance company keeps the premium paid for taking on the risk.

In the same way, with a Put option, you can insure a stock by fixing a selling price; If something happens to cause the stock price to fall, you can exercise your option and sell it at its insured price; however, if the stock's price goes up and there is no uncertainty, then you do not need the insurance; and your only expense would have been the premium.

Following are some basic terms that one should know before trading options:

Strike Price

The predetermined price that the buyer and the seller of an option have agreed on is called the Strike Price; in other words, the price at which the option is to be exercised is called Strike Price or Exercise Price.

Premium

Option premium is the upfront payment made by the buyer to the seller to get the privileges of an option contract. The price of an Option Premium is based on two factors – intrinsic value and time value of the option.

Intrinsic Value

Intrinsic Value is the difference between the current market price and the strike price of an option. It can either be positive or zero.

Time Value

The amount of time left in a contract affects its price. The closer the contract is to its expiration date the lesser value it has and the price of the premium will fall. This means that if the time left between the current date and the expiration date of Contract X is longer than that of Contract Y, Contract X has higher time value.

In the money

Call Option - underlying instrument price is higher than the strike price.

Put Option - underlying instrument price is lower than the strike price.

Out of the money

Call Option - underlying instrument price is lower than the strike price.

Put Option - underlying instrument price is higher than the strike price.

At the money

The underlying price is equivalent to the strike price.

'Options' is a vast topic and it cannot be explained in a few pages. So, I will give a detailed explanation about one strategy where the winning probability is very high; readers who have years of experience doing options can try their hands on this. As always, first paper trade and only then trade with your real account.

Naked options writing

Options traders frequently start their trading careers as options buyers. When you are an option buyer you have to be right about market direction and about the amount of time it will take the market to move. Since time value works against them the winning probability is only twenty five percent.

Most retail customers don't know that it is possible to be on the other side of the trade - where the winning probability is seventy five percent.

An options writer sells the option contract that option buyers are paying for.

The option seller is taking on the exact opposite responsibility of the option buyer. If the option buyer wants to exercise their option, the writer has an obligation to deliver.

Remember, an option buyer has limited risk and unlimited profit potential whereas an option writer has unlimited risk and limited profit potential.

Why writing options has a higher winning probability?

Generally seventy to ninety five percent of all options expire worthless; what this means is that by buying an option (calls or puts) the odds of losing are significantly higher; so, options sellers make money by allowing the contract to expire worthless.

Consider the following to write short-term options that are seventy five percent in your favor.

Writing options has three out of four chances of winning.

Example:

Sell ALBK 80 Call for Rs.7 when stock is trading at Rs. 70

Possibilities:

If the stock price goes below Rs.80 - win (Out of The Money)

If the stock price equal to Rs.80 - win (At The Money)

If the stock price goes up a little bit but not > Rs.87 - win (In The Money)

If the stock price goes up a lot > Rs.87 - lose (In The Money)

By using the above method, we have possibility of winning three out of four times. There is no uncertainty, because ROI (Return on Investment), max profit and the time to exit are determined at the point of entry itself.

Points to remember:

1. Write naked calls in bear markets; naked puts in bull markets.
2. Write options that are at least twenty five percent overpriced.

3. Write options that are at least twenty percent out of the money.
4. Select stocks with low price volatility.
5. As a retail investor, the opportunity to sell options and earn premium is always open to you. But, remember that the risks are unlimited when you sell options. Ensure that you have adequate capital to handle margins. Buying an option is straightforward, but selling options is a totally different ball game. You have to pay the MTM (Mark to Market) margin every day if the stock price goes against you.
6. Most importantly, place the order online yourself and not through a broker over phone. Because, in India most brokers are very new to selling options and they may place a wrong order.

Advantages of writing/selling options:

1. You get paid upfront in the form of premium (potential profit).
2. When the option expires out of the money - which often happens - then no one will want to exercise the contract and you can keep the entire premium as profit.
3. Time decay reduces liability and risk for options sellers, because one has already sold the option for a higher price and has taken the premium.

4. You can close your contract at any time by buying the option back. This can be done at any time during market hours.

Common Mistakes that option sellers make

Option selling is a passive activity that requires time and patience. Following are the most common mistakes that a trader makes when it comes to selling options:

Mistake One: No exit plan

In option selling, it is difficult to decide when to close the position. There are times that options will expire worthless, but it is simply not worth the risk. The important thing is that you should have an exit plan.

Mistake two: Over-positioning

Over-positioning is the biggest mistake new option sellers make. No matter how much training one undergoes on how to sell options, it is difficult to coach somebody on how to position. New traders sell a few options, see them decay and get excited thinking they have found a smart way to earn money. They start selling too many options relative to their account size and end up with too many options. This puts the whole portfolio at greater risk of taking losses. Option selling works seventy five percent in our favor but one has to understand and respect the leverage.

Mistake three: Selling too close to the money

Many option sellers think that the best way to sell options is to select a strike price that has only a few days remaining until expiration. The reasoning is that you get the maximum rate of time decay. To get good premium one has to sell quite close to the money (selling perilously close); but this is not a good practice because 'in the money' options appreciate quickly. Remember, staying 'out of the money' is one key way to avoid a big loss.

Rule of thumb

1. Maximum loss per trade - not more than two percent of capital.
   Example: If 10 lakhs is your capital, maximum allowed loss/trade should not be more than two percent; i.e., maximum allowed loss per trade should not be greater than Rs.20,000.

2. How to decide the quantity to trade?
   Quantity to trade = (loss per trade/risk per trade) Risk per trade is the maximum a share can move in a day. Say, this is Rs.20, then quantity to trade = 20000/20=1000 nos.

3. Jot down your bad trades and mistakes - a journal will be very useful for future reference. This will help you to learn from your mistakes.
4. Do not chase the market.
5. Take your profit when it is on your platter.

Difference between futures and options:

Futures	Options
Requires high margin payment than options.	Requires only the premium amount. This is very less when compared to the margin money paid for futures.
Unlimited profit and loss.	Unlimited profit and limited loss.
Preferred by speculators.	Preferred by hedgers.
Buyer is obligated to honor contract.	There is no obligation for the buyer to buy / sell.

Conclusion:

Warren Buffet refers to derivatives as 'financial weapons of mass destruction'. It means that F&O can create huge losses that can be very difficult to recover. They might lead to capital erosion. Even though F&O has certain advantages, stay away from them till you gain good knowledge.

CHAPTER 4

IPO (Initial Public Offering)

IPO is the first sale of stock offered by a private company to the public. It is sometimes referred to as 'a company going public'. IPO opens up opportunity for any individual to invest in the company.

Generally, companies do an IPO to raise capital for expansion. Private companies can raise capital by borrowing from banks and finding private investors; but companies take the IPO route to get a huge capital at very less cost.

Any private registered company can come out with an IPO, provided it fulfils all the criteria specified by the stock exchange. The entire IPO process is controlled by SEBI (Securities and Exchange Board of India).

The company wishing to go public must develop an impressive management and professional team who will be able to steer the company in the right path, once goes public.

Once a company fulfils all the eligibility criteria for IPO it has to go through the following steps to list itself in National Stock Exchange:

Step 1: Appointing an Underwriter
Investment banks like HDFC and ICICI act as underwriters on behalf of the company. One or more banks are appointed for the unbiased execution of the IPO process.

Step 2: Registering in SEBI and preparing Red Herring Prospectus
To start the IPO process, a company registers under SEBI and submits the relevant documents such as basic KYC details and the financial statements for official audit. Once SEBI is satisfied, the Red Herring Prospectus is prepared.

Red Herring Prospectus contains details such as sales, assets, revenue and relevant financial data of the company. Appointed underwriter sends this to SEBI for approval.

Step 3: Marketing
If SEBI approves, the underwriter advertises the company to promote the IPO. Advertisements are usually done through business magazines and newspapers.

Step 4: Deciding the price

Investment banks help the company to decide the price of its security. Price is fixed or discovered using a book building process. In the book building process, the underwriter sets up a price band and lets investors bid. Price is then fixed depending on the demand from investors.

Step 5: Getting listed

Finally a date is set for listing in the exchange. From that day the stock starts to trade in the secondary market.

Step 6: Refund, if any

All investors will not be allocated shares if the demand is high. Investors who do not get an allotment are refunded their money.

Three categories of investors:

1. Qualified Institutional Buyers
2. Non Institutional Investors
3. Retail Investors

Qualified Institutional Buyers (QIB)

Financial institutions such as banks, mutual funds, insurance companies and Foreign Institutional Investors (FIIs) fall under this category. A maximum of fifty percent of the issue can be reserved for investors falling under the QIB category. Out of this, five percent can be reserved for Mutual Funds.

Non Institutional Investors

This is also called the High Net worth Individual (HNI) quota. Resident Indian Individuals, Hindu Undivided Families (HUF), companies, NRIs, Societies and trusts whose shares application bid is more than Rs. 1 lakh fall under this category. At least fifteen percent of the total issue can be reserved for this group.

Retail Investors

Individuals, both residents and NRIs, along with HUF fall under this category. The application size should be less than Rs. 1 lakh. A minimum of thirty percent of the issue has to be reserved for such people.

What is meant by oversubscribed?

Generally an IPO is considered to be oversubscribed when the demand is more than the total number of shares that are available.

An IPO can get oversubscribed in all categories. I will explain this with an example under the retail investor's category.

Example:

A company X comes up with an IPO and offers 20 lakh shares to retail investors. Let's assume that 40,000 investors apply for 100 shares each – the total requirement here is 40 lakh shares whereas there are only 20 lakh shares available. Hence the issue is said to be oversubscribed by two times in the retail investor category.

How retail category allotment happens when the issue is oversubscribed?

Many investors are under the misconception that allotment of IPO is based on preference to time and quantity, among others; but this is not true. According to the rules laid down by SEBI, the company cannot allot lower than the minimum lot size to anyone; so the company tries to allot minimum lot size of shares to everyone who has applied, regardless of how many lots a person has applied for. The remaining shares are distributed proportionately to those who have bid for higher than the minimum lot. If you have bid for shares worth Rs.1.5 lakh, you will receive the minimum lot, plus shares proportionate to your bid.

Sometimes, the total number of shares bid for - in minimum lots - is bigger than the issue size. In that case, the minimum lots are allotted based on a computerised random draw. This is like a lucky draw and it's quite possible that an applicant who applied for a minimum lot gets his allocation, whereas someone who has applied for more number of lots gets nothing. Thus, it is clear that bidding for the maximum lot does not increase your chances of getting an allotment.

Do's:

1. Read the Prospectus/ Abridged Prospectus and pay special attention to risk factors.
2. Investigate the purpose of the issue.
3. Check the company's history.
4. Check the background of the promoters.
5. To increase chances of allotment apply from the accounts of various family members.

Don't's:

1. Don't fall prey to market rumours.
2. Don't go by any implicit/explicit promise made by the issuer or anyone else.
3. Don't invest based on the prevailing bull run of the market index.

Pros and Cons of an IPO

Pros:

1. Gives the company a lower cost of capital.
2. Increases the company's exposure, prestige, and public image, which can help the company's sales and profits.
3. Public companies can attract and retain better management and skilled employees through liquid equity participation (e.g. ESOPs).

4. Facilitating acquisitions (potentially in return for shares of stock).
5. Raises the largest amount of money for the company compared to other options.

Cons:

1. Company is required to disclose financial, accounting, tax, and other business information.
2. Significant legal, accounting and marketing costs. Increased time, effort and attention required from management for reporting.
3. Public dissemination of information which may be useful to competitors, suppliers and customers.
4. Loss of control and stronger agency problems because of new shareholders who obtain voting rights and can effectively control company decisions via the board of directors.
5. Increased risk of legal or regulatory issues such as private securities, class action lawsuits and shareholder actions.

What is 'ASBA'?

ASBA is "Application Supported by Blocked Amount". ASBA is an application containing an authorization to block the application money in the bank account- for subscribing to an IPO or Rights Issue. If an investor is applying through ASBA, his application money can be debited from the bank account only after allotment is finalized.

Submission of ASBA application form

Investors can submit the ASBA application form to the trading member or to a SCSB (Self Certified Syndicate Banks). List of all SCSBs and their branches where ASBA application forms can be submitted is available on the SEBI and NSE website. Investors need not necessarily have their DP account with the SCSB where they are submitting the form.

Or

Investors can submit the ASBA application to their stock broker.

Or

Apply online through internet banking facility - if provided by your SCSB/Trading member.

Most retail investors submit the filled ASBA form to their SCSB banking branch. In turn, the bank will upload the details of the application in the bidding platform. The application contains all the required details such as name of the applicant, PAN number, demat account number, bid quantity and bid price.

Eligibility criteria to apply through ASBA

All the investors can apply for IPO through ASBA. In case of rights issues, all shareholders of the company - as on record date - are permitted to use ASBA only if:

- They are holding shares in dematerialised form and have applied for entitlements or additional shares in the issue in dematerialised form.
- He/She is not a renouncee.

Why stocks price declines after a few months of the IPO?

In some cases, a few months after the ipo the stock price takes a steep downturn. This is often because of the expiration of the lock-up period. When a company goes public, the underwriters make company insiders such as officials and employees sign a lock-up agreement. A lock-up agreement is a legal binding contract between the underwriters and insiders of the company prohibiting them from selling any shares for a specified period of time. The period ranges from ninety days to twenty-four months. The problem is that when the lock-up period is over, all the insiders are permitted to sell their stock; as a result many people start selling to book profits; and this kind of sudden excess supply can bring the stock price down.

Advantage an investor has in applying through ASBA

Applying through ASBA facility has the following advantages:

(i) The investor continues to earn interest on the application money as it remains in the bank account.
(ii) ASBA is convenient and reduces time while applying for IPOs.
(iii) The investor does not have to bother about refunds since in ASBA only the money required for allotment of securities is taken from the bank account; and that too only when his application is selected for allotment after the basis of allotment is finalized.
(iv) Five applications can be made from a bank account per issue.

Websites showing IPO allotment results:

Whenever one applies for an IPO, NSE/BSE will send an SMS/mail about the allotment status; but their messages are sometimes delayed by a couple of days. Check the status on the following websites to immediately know your status once the allotment is done:

- Link intime (https://linkintime.co.in/PublicIssues/)
- Karvy (http://ipo.karvy.com/)

You just have to enter any one of the following in the webpage to know the allotment status.

- PAN Card number
- IPO application number
- DP ID/ Client ID

IPO funding

These days most IPOs get oversubscribed and the chances of allotment for individuals are very less. To maximize the chance of allotment one has to apply in the HNI category (a retail investor who applies for more than Rs 2,00,000 worth of shares in an IPO is considered an HNI).

IPO financing/funding is a loan offered by NBFCs (Non Banking Financial Company) mainly to HNI (High Net worth Individuals) for applying IPOs.

Investors who opt for IPO funding usually sell the allotted shares on the day of listing (flipping strategy) and do not hold for a long period.

Anyone applying for IPO funding has to pay just the margin money and the rest of the funds are loaned by the NBFC.

The interest rates are very less ranging from eight to twelve percent per annum.

IPO funding is for a very short period - about seven to fifteen days; and the repayment tenure is up to three months.

For a first time investor, the process of IPO funding may be a bit scary; because the documentation takes time and most NBFCs require shares to be pledged; moreover they charge processing fee and stamp duty for loan agreement.

Step by step procedure in an IPO funding:

1. Open a financing account with an NBFC (one time procedure).
2. Fill the required forms, give power of attorney and submit all the relevant documents (one time procedure).
3. Give details of the IPO that you are interested in.
4. Pay the margin money.
5. Remaining funds will be disbursed by the NBFC within one working day.
6. If an allotment happens then the allotted shares will get credited to your demat account.
7. Investor advises the NBFC to sell the shares.
8. Finally investor books profit/loss and settles the loan amount.

NBFCs involved in IPO financing

The following are the NBFC s involved in IPO funding:

1. ShareKhan
2. Aditya Birla Money
3. Axis Finance Ltd
4. SMC Finance
5. Edelweiss
6. JM Financial

They usually fund from Rs. 2 lakhs to Rs. 25 crores.

Pros and Cons of IPO funding

Pros:

1. IPO funding allows investors to participate in the HNI category even if they don't have sufficient funds.
2. Securities held in your demat account can be used as margin money.

Cons:

1. Good IPOs usually get oversubscribed and the quantity of allotted shares will be less. Even though the shares gets listed at a premium price, the profit earned will be very less when compared to the cost of getting the IPO funding.

2. Sometimes the shares get allotted and if the list price is below the subscription price then the investor ends up in loss. The investor not only loses the buy/sell price difference but also the expenses incurred to receive the IPO funding; so the loss gets magnified.

CHAPTER 5

Dematerialisation

The Indian stock market has a history of more than 100 years and until the 1996 all the shares were held in the form of physical certificates.

A share certificate is a written document representing ownership in a company; they contain the following information:

- Name of the share holder
- Number of shares owned
- Date
- Folio number
- Distinctive number
- Certificate number
- Face value
- Corporate seal and signatures.

Usually, the certificates have intricate designs to discourage fraudulent replication. The following snapshot illustrates this point.

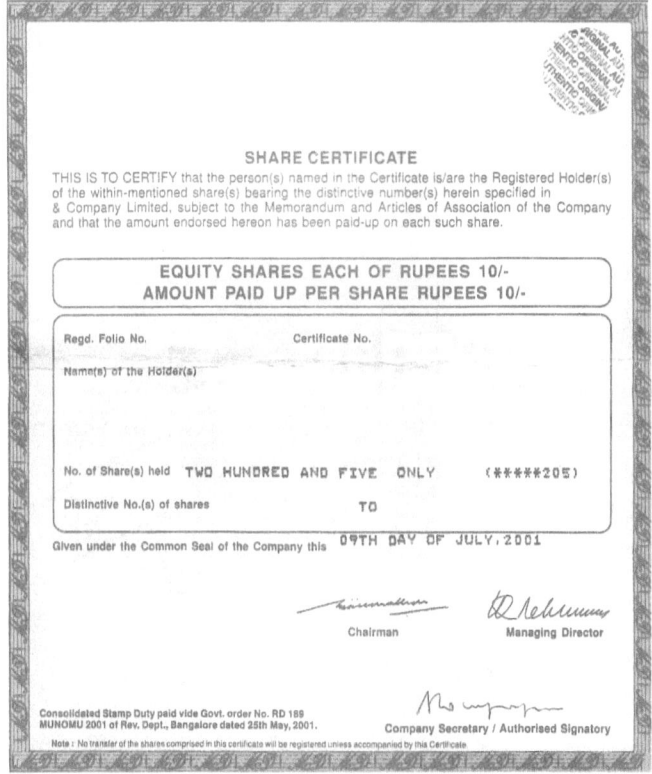

Sample physical share certificate

What is a Demat Account?

A Demat Account holds securities (shares, bonds and debentures) in an electronic form. It is similar to a savings bank account because, instead of currencies, securities are held by notional value in electronic form.

A Demat Account can be opened with any one of the following two depositories:

NSDL - National Securities Depository Limited or

CDSL - Central Depository Services Limited

A retail investors cannot directly open a Demat Account with these depositories; they have to go through intermediaries called Depository Participants (DPs). Today, many banks and brokers act as depository participants.

Dematerialisation

Dematerialisation/demat is the process of converting physical shares into electronic format. Dematerialisation of shares is optional and an investor can hold shares in the physical form. The drawback is that if he wishes to sell it on the stock exchange, most brokers will not accept it.

Any investor who wants to dematerialise his shares needs to open a demat account with a depository participant (DP); once the account is opened a unique client id is generated and the following needs to be done:

Step by step procedure to dematerialise physical shares

- Open a demat account with a Depository Participant (DP); a Depository Participant is an agent who interacts with the depository (i.e. NSDL / CDSL) Banks or broking house act as Depository Participants.
- Fill up a Dematerialisation Request Form (DRF) provided by the DP and submit it to the Depository Participant along with the physical share certificates.
- The DP, upon receipt of the share certificate and the DRF, will send an electronic request to the company's registrar and share-transfer agent (RTA) through the depository - for confirmation of the demat. Each request will bear a unique transaction number called Dematerialisation Request Number (DRN).
- Then these share certificates will be marked with a 'Surrendered for Dematerialisation' seal.

- The company's registrar and share transfer agent will verify the documents and will then confirm the demat to the depository.
- The DP will hold the shares on your behalf in the dematerialised form and you will be the beneficial owner of the dematerialised shares.

Sample Dematerialisation Request Form

Normal Dematerialisation or
Transmission-cum- Dematerialisation
or Transposition-cum-Dematerialisation

Depository Participant Name / Address

(To be filled up by the Depository Participant)

DRN		Date	D	D	M	M	Y	Y	Y	Y
DRF No.		Date	D	D	M	M	Y	Y	Y	Y

(To be filled by the BO. Please fill all the details in BLOCK LETTERS in English. Fill up a separate DRF for Free securities and Locked – in securities. In case of locked - in securities fill up a separate DRF for different lock-in reason / lock-in expiry dates.)

I / We request you to dematerialise the enclosed security certificate(s) registered in my / our name into my / our demat account.

DP ID							Client ID							
Name of the Company														
ISIN	I	N												
Quantity to be Dematerialised	(In Figures)													
	(In Words)													
Number Of Certificates (in words)														
Nature of Securities		☐ Free Securities ☐ Lock-in Securities												
Lock-in reason														
Lock in Expiry Date		D	D	M	M	Y	Y	Y	Y					

Details of Securities:						
Type of Security	☐ Equity ☐ Debentures ☐ Bonds ☐ Units ☐ Other (Specify)					
Face Value of Securities						
	From	To	From	To	From	To
Folio No.						
Certificate Numbers						
Distinctive Numbers						
Quantity						

Attach an annexure (duly signed by account holder(s)) in the above format if the space is not sufficient.

The original certificates / documents are hereby surrendered by me / us for dematerialisation and the same are free from any lien or charge or encumbrance and represent the bonafide securities of the Issuer Company to the best of my / our knowledge and belief.

	First / Sole Holder	Second Holder	Third Holder
Name			
Signature with DP			
Signature with RTA			

Participant Authorization (From DP to RTA)

We have received the above-mentioned securities bearing ISIN_____ for Dematerialisation. The Application form is verified with the Certificates / Documents surrendered for dematerialisation and we certify that the application form is in accordance with the details mentioned in the enclosed certificates / documents. It is also certified that the Holder(s) of securities have a beneficiary account with us in the same name(s) and order of name(s).

                        Depository Participant Seal and Signature

Acknowledgement Receipt

DRF No.				Date	D	D	M	M	Y	Y	Y	Y
DP ID						Client ID						
First / Sole Holder Name												
Second Joint Holder Name												
Third Joint Holder Name												
Name of the Company												
Type of Security	☐ Equity ☐ Debentures ☐ Bonds ☐ Units ☐ Other (Specify)											
ISIN												
No. of Securities (in figures)												
No. of securities (in words)												
No. of Certificates (in figures)												
No. of Certificates (in words)												

We hereby acknowledge the receipt of certificates / documents, in respect of the following securities for dematerialisation subject to verification: -

Depository Participant Seal and Signature

Most common reasons for demat rejection

Sometimes dematerialisation requests get rejected for any one of the following reasons:

1. If there is a change in face value.

2. Change in companies name due to merger or for other reasons.
3. Signature mismatch.
4. Physical quantity of shares received by R&T agent is more than the quantity mentioned in the demat request form.
5. On submission of fake certificates.
6. If certificates received are reported as lost/stolen and a stop is recorded in computer master files.
7. If a stop is recorded as per bank lien or court order.
8. If ISIN in certificate does not relate to the one mentioned in DRF.

Special case 1

When the demat account holder's name doesn't match the name mentioned in the physical share certificate.

Sometimes, the clients name might not match the name appearing on the certificate; this could be on account of initials – e.g. suffixed instead of affixed, initials not spelled out, etc. Such cases will still be processed if the signature of the client on the Demat Request Form (DRF) matches the specimen signature available with the Issuers / R & T agent.

Example:

The shareholder may have opened the demat account in the name of Kumar Navaneethan Madhusudhanan, but his name on the share certificate may appear as K.N. Madhusudhanan or Kumar N Madhusudhanan; such requests will be treated as good for dematerialisation, provided the DP verifies the signature and finds that it matches.

Special case 2
Deletion of name, in case of joint holding, and dematerialisation can be done at the same time.

On the death of any one of the account member of a joint holding, the surviving joint holder can get the name of the deceased deleted from the physical certificate and get the securities dematerialised.

The following steps need to be taken:

Submit a DRF along with the share certificates and relevant documents - such as death certificate, address and ID proof of nominee and transmission form for deleting the name of the deceased - to the DP. On receipt of the documents mentioned above, the DP will forward the same to the Issuer or its R & T Agent.

After proper vetting, the Issuer or its R & T Agent carry out the name deletion and then process the dematerialisation request.

Special case 3
Demat process for physical share certificates of a deceased family member.

Sometimes family members are left with physical share certificates held by the deceased.

Before approaching the companies check for the following:

- If the shares were held by the individual or jointly with someone.
- If there is any nomination registered on the share certificate.
- If the company still exists.
- If the company's name has changed.
- Did the company merge with any another company?
- Is there any change in face value?

After the above mentioned preliminary checks, approach the company's Registrar and Transfer agent. Submit a written application enclosing the physical certificates and attested copy of the death certificate. Joint holders, if any, should sign the request letter. In case of nomination, include a copy of identity and address proof of the nominee. In case of no nominations, the legal heir should submit probate of will or legal heir certificate attested by a notary.

After checking all the documents, the company will issue the physical share certificate in the name of the new holders (nominees/joint holders/legal heirs/

legatee). This new certificate can be submitted for dematerialisation.

How to find the transfer agent of a particular company?

Option 1
https://www.nseindia.com/corporates/corporateHome.html?id=companyDetails

Click on the link above and enter the company's name that you wish to get information about.

Note: Due to the dynamic nature of the Internet, the link provided may or may not work.

Option 2
Type the company's name in Google and obtain the company's website and on their website, click the contact us tab.

Advantages of dematerialisation

Dealing in demat format is beneficial for investors, brokers and companies.

There are several benefits associated with the demat system.

1. It is a safe and convenient way to hold securities.
2. It ensures immediate transfer of securities.
3. There is no stamp duty on transfer of securities.
4. Risks associated with physical certificates such as bad delivery, fake securities, delays and thefts are eliminated.
5. There is a major reduction in paperwork involved in transfer of securities; and there is considerable reduction in transaction cost.
6. No odd lot problem exists; even a single share can be sold.
7. Change in address recorded with DP automatically gets registered with all companies in which the investor holds securities eliminating the need to correspond with each and every company separately.
8. Correspondence with the companies is not necessary as the DP transmits the securities.
9. When corporate actions like bonus/split/consolidation/merger occur the shares are automatically credited into the demat account.
10. Holding investments in equity, and debt instruments - in a single account, is possible.
11. Appointment of nominee is easy in DP thereby eliminating correspondence with each and every company.

12. There's no need to go to the broker for taking delivery or submitting the share certificates.
13. Liquidity is very high.
14. Interest on loan against demat shares are less when compared to physical shares.
15. One needs to pay less brokerage in case of dematerialised shares.

CHAPTER 6

Delisting

Delisting is the removal of listed securities of a company from a stock exchange. Once a company is delisted, the securities of that company will no longer be traded at that stock exchange. It happens either as a voluntary decision by the company or is forcibly enforced by SEBI on account of some wrongdoing by the company.

Delisting can happen in two different ways:

- Voluntary delisting
- Compulsory delisting

Voluntary delisting

In voluntary delisting, a company decides, on its own, to remove its securities from the stock exchange in which it was traded. There are three positive reasons why a company would choose to delist itself.

Reason 1
Going private consolidates the ownership of a company and can actually put the company in a better financial position.

Reason 2
Corporate restructuring is another reason for delisting; companies may change their names as a result of a merger or an acquisition.

Reason 3:
Companies choose to move to another major exchange.

In any of these cases, delisting is not a reason for alarm.

Compulsory delisting

In compulsory delisting, the securities of a company are removed from a stock exchange by SEBI as a penal measure on account of some wrongdoing by the company.

Companies can be delisted by SEBI for the following reasons:

Reason 1
All major stock exchanges have strict filing requirement for listed companies; this ensures transparency in the company's financials and accounting. Considering these financial ratios, investors take decisions on whether to buy or not. When companies don't meet their reporting deadlines, they get delisted.

Reason 2
Another factor that determines whether or not a company will retain the privilege of being listed on the exchange is stock performance.

The Nasty Side of Delisting

As per the new delisting norms framed by the Securities and Exchange Board of India, re-listing of a company can be done only after ten years - if the delisting is compulsory. In case of voluntary delisting, however, the companies can list themselves again after a period of five years. A few years ago, the gap between delisting and relisting was only two years, but now the laws have been tightened.

Exceptional cases - small companies and those getting delisted because they are winding-up operations can get listed again after a period of five years.

What delisting means to shareholders and how to sell the delisted shares to the promoters?

Ownership of stock in a delisted company will never change; you will still own those shares and retain the right to vote. When you own delisted stock, cutting your losses might seem like a good move. But, unless your holding amount is huge it might not be worth the time and fees.

SEBI has two exit opportunities when a company gets delisted:

- In case of voluntary delisting, the exit price is determined through the Reverse Book Building process. The floor price will be announced and the shareholders have to make a bid at a price either on or above the floor price. If the exit price, as a result of bidding, is acceptable to the promoter, the promoter pays that price to the investors and the investors can exit.
- Those investors who missed the Reverse Book Building process have an option to offer their shares for sale to the promoters within a period of one year from the date of closure of the delisting process. The promoters are under an obligation to accept the shares at the same exit price.

How to sell shares that are not traded anymore?

If you own illiquid/delisted shares that you are not able to sell in the open market, don't worry, because there are several companies/dealers who buy such shares.

To evaluate a company whose shares are not traded is tough. To arrive at the price the dealers collect data from the Internet, data base of stock exchanges, courts, the BIFR website and companies themselves.

However, there's a catch - because there is no exchange for such shares, the price is determined by the dealer and is usually forty to fifty percent less than the valuation of companies in the same business that they are listed in. The dealers use the same parameters that are used to value a listed company; however, the price is at times negotiable. Generally, the scope of price negotiation is up to ten percent, but it depends on the stock.

Why a dealer purchases delisted shares?

There are some dealers who buy delisted shares and you may wonder why these dealers show interest in buying these delisted shares. These dealers advertise their willingness to buy these shares at a premium (more than the open offer price that the company bought). This is because the valuation of the company may have gone up several notches since it got delisted. In case the company lists again, a share will be worth a lot more than the price at which it got delisted.

Example 1

OMDC (Orissa Minerals Development Company) is one of the oldest iron ore mining companies in India and its shares were available for Rs 2.50 per share when it was listed in the Calcutta stock exchange. Since these exchanges were not working, the shares remained illiquid.

It got listed on the Bombay Stock Exchange (BSE) in August 2010. It made a stellar debut hitting a price of Rs 20,475 per share.

The stock rose to Rs 92,200 in 2010. Though the company was listed all this while on the Calcutta Stock Exchange, trading did not take off due to stringent margin requirements. The stock started trading actively only after being listed on the BSE.

Example 2

Pilani Investment and Industries Corporation is an investment arm of the BK Birla Group. The stock was listed on the Madhya Pradesh Stock Exchange where it was barely liquid. It was listed on BSE and NSE on October 26, 2011; on debut, it touched Rs 2,535 during the day. It was changing hands at Rs 1,500 per share in off-market transactions.

Pilani Investment was listed on regional exchanges. Since these exchanges were not working, the shares remained illiquid till they were listed on BSE and NSE.

Conclusion

- Dealers show more interest in buying voluntarily delisted shares.
- The profit may be attractive, but the loss will be devastating.

The below link shows the list of delisted companies:
http://www.bseindia.com/corporates/Delist_Comp.aspx?expandable=1

http://www.smctradeonline.com/company-delisted-shares.aspx

Disclaimer: Due to the dynamic nature of the Internet the links mentioned may have changed and no longer be valid.

CHAPTER 7

Hindu Undivided Family (HUF): a Less Known Tax Saving Tool

HUF (Hindu Undivided Family)

Any individual who is covered by Hindu personal law can create an HUF account. This means that individuals belonging to other religions, other than Jains and Sikhs, are not allowed to form HUF. As an exception, Jains and Sikhs are allowed to create HUF even though they are not governed by the Hindu law. Any married Hindu individual is eligible to open an HUF account.

A person can split his taxable income between his individual self and his HUF; i.e., he can claim double benefits for deductions and expenses in both PANs, thereby substantially reducing his overall tax liability.

MEMBERS OF HUF

A single person cannot form an HUF, it is formed by a family. An HUF consists of the following persons:

Karta

Karta of a HUF is the senior most male member of the family. Everything will be authorized by the Karta (the father usually takes the responsibility) and he takes all the decisions on behalf of the family. Signature of the Karta with seal will be required for all bank transactions.

Coparcener

A coparcener is a person who acquires a right in the ancestral property by birth and a person who has a right to demand partition in the HUF property. Not all members of the HUF are its coparceners - sons, daughters, grandsons and great grandsons, can be coparceners.

How to create an HUF?

It is not necessary to create HUF on the day of marriage itself; it can be created at any point of time in the future – it's not a difficult task.

The following three things are required to create an HUF:

1. HUF Deed
2. HUF PAN Card (Mandatory)
3. HUF Bank Account (Mandatory)

HUF DEED

The HUF deed is a written formal document on a stamp paper stating the names of the Karta and the coparceners of the HUF.

It's a declaration containing the following:

1. The Karta holds the right to govern all the transactions of the HUF account on behalf of the members.
2. The names of all the members of the HUF are stated in the HUF deed.

The name of the HUF is usually the name of the Karta followed by the word HUF. For e.g., if the Karta of the HUF is Kumar, then the name of his HUF account will be Kumar HUF.

Creating a HUF Deed is not mandatory; PAN card and bank account can be opened without a HUF deed, but it's better to have a written document in place.

HUF PAN CARD

Since HUF is a separate entity, a separate PAN card is required. The application for an HUF PAN Card can be applied online as well as manually.

HUF PAN Card applications can be made online through the below mentioned link: https://www.onlineservices.nsdl.com/paam/endUserRegisterContact.html

The PAN Card application has to be signed by the Karta.

HUF BANK ACCOUNT

An HUF bank account can be opened in any bank. While opening an HUF bank account, a rubber stamp of the HUF will be required, because the application form requires signature with a seal. Apart from this, residential proof and identification proof of Karta need to be submitted.

Once the HUF deed, HUF PAN card and HUF bank accounts are ready, one can start receiving payments in the name of the HUF.

HOW TO CREATE HUF CAPITAL?

There are many ways to infuse capital in an HUF. One of the most effective and popular methods of creating

HUF capital is by receiving gifts without attracting any tax. Following are the ways to create HUF capital as advised by a CA:

1. Gifts from relatives of the members of HUF. As per Section 56(ii) of the Income Tax Act, gifts received from relatives of the members of HUF is fully exempted from tax.
2. Gifts received at the time of marriage of any member of the HUF are fully exempted from the levy of Income Tax.
3. Any ancestral property can be transferred to the HUF to create capital.
4. Gifts from strangers that are less than Rs. 50,000. If the value of gifts received from a stranger during a financial year does not exceed Rs. 50,000, then this amount is exempted from tax. Remember, there is no limit on gifts received from family members.

Different sources of income permitted to be shown under HUF

The HUF can earn income from all sources (except salary) and the income so earned would help the HUF create more capital. Following are the sources of income for a HUF:

1. Business income.

2. By investing in shares and mutual funds.
3. Rental income
4. Interest earned from fixed deposits.
5. By buying and selling properties.

Tax benefits on a HUF account:

Following are the various tax benefits a family can avail:

1. Tax rebates and deductions can be availed under section 80C for an HUF account.
2. HUF money accumulated can be used to take life insurance policies of its members.
3. HUF can pay salary to its members if they are contributing to the functioning of the family business. This expense towards salary can be deducted from the HUF's income.
4. Investments can be made from the HUF's income; for example, one can even open a demat account under HUF and start investing in equity.
5. Gifts from relatives of the members of HUF are exempted from the levy of tax.

How to save tax by forming HUF?

The logic behind forming an HUF is to save tax and to avail the benefits of an additional PAN Card.

The following example shows how to save tax with the help of HUF pan:

Example

Consider a family with husband, wife and a son. The income of the husband is Rs. 30 lakhs and income of the wife is Rs. 20 lakhs. They also have an ancestral property from which they are earning rent of Rs. 9 lakhs p.a. If they don't have a HUF, this property rent will either be taxed in the hands of the husband or wife or both.

If taxed in the hands of the husband

Since his individual income is 30 lakhs, he comes under the thirty percent income tax slab and would be required to pay thirty percent on the rental income of Rs. 9 lakhs i.e. Rs. 2.7 lakhs as tax.

If taxed in the hands of the wife

Since her individual income is 20 lakhs, she also comes under the thirty percent income tax slab and would be required to pay thirty percent on the rental income of Rs. 9 lakhs i.e. Rs. 2.7 lakhs as tax.

If taxed equally in the hands of both husband and wife

If each gets Rs.4.5 lakhs as rental income, both the husband and wife have to pay tax of thirty percent on Rs. 4.5 lakh. This means each will pay a tax 1.35 lakhs, so the total tax paid on rental income is Rs. 2.7 lakhs.

If taxed under HUF

If this rental income of Rs. 9 lakhs is taxed in the hands of HUF, the tax payable would be only Rs. 90,000 as the total income is less than 10 lakhs – ten percent income tax slab category will be applicable.

Thus, it is evident that taxing the family rental income in the hands of the HUF would lead to a tax saving of Rs. 1,80,000 p.a. (Rs. 2,70,000 – Rs. 90,000).

OTHER RELEVANT POINTS REGARDING HUF

1. HUF has to file income tax return every year just like an individual.
2. Due date for filing of income tax return of the HUF is usually 31st July of the assessment year. However, in case of tax audit the due date of filing of return would then be 30th September.
3. The Karta of the HUF has the power to sign all documents on behalf of the family members.

However, he may also permit other adult members to have this power.

4. An adopted child can become a member of the HUF but he cannot become a coparcener. The difference between a member and a coparcener is that the member cannot ask for partition of the HUF.
5. HUFs are recognised all over India, except in Kerala.
6. For creating the HUF one needs to get married, but it is not necessary to have children.
7. A stranger can gift the HUF, but not more than Rs. 50,000.
8. Daughters can continue to be a coparceners of her parental family's HUF and also of her husband's HUF; that way daughters can be coparancers in two HUFs.
9. An HUF demat can be opened and the capital from the HUF savings can be used to trade and invest in equity.
10. While applying for an IPO, one can apply using his individual pan as well as the HUF pan. This increases the probability of allocation of shares.

Disadvantages of HUF account

1. Any common property cannot be sold without the concurrence of all the members. All members of the family have a right in the assets

of the Hindu Undivided Family (including an unborn child in the womb of a mother). An HUF can get too large to manage.
2. Opening an HUF is easy but closing it down is difficult; the only way an HUF can be dissolved is by a partition; all members have to agree to dissolve the HUF. Under a partition, assets are distributed to members that can lead to a lot of disputes and legal issues.
3. Divorce rates are rising and therefore, HUF as a tax vehicle is losing importance.
4. Once an HUF is formed, you must continue to file its tax returns unless a partition takes place.

Conclusion

Remember, a penny saved is a penny earned. HUF is the legal way to to save tax by obtaining an extra PAN card for the family.

HUF is beneficial for those who have a huge income and ancestral assets. Though HUF seems like the perfect way to save tax as a family, it comes with its own limitations and drawbacks. Seek the advice of a CA before opting for an HUF.

CHAPTER 8

Famous Quotes by Legends

Warren Buffet quotes:

"If you don't find a way to make money while you sleep, you will work until you die."

"Time is the friend of the wonderful company, the enemy of the mediocre."

"Someone's sitting in the shade today because someone planted a tree a long time ago."

"Calling someone who trades actively in the market an investor is like calling someone who repeatedly engages in one-night stands a romantic."

"Successful investing takes time, discipline and patience. No matter how great the talent or effort, some things just take time: You can't produce a baby in one month by getting nine women pregnant."

"Opportunities come infrequently. When it rains gold, put out the bucket, not the thimble"

"It is not necessary to do extraordinary things to get extraordinary results."

"It's far better to buy a wonderful company at a fair price than a fair company at a wonderful price"

"Most people get interested in stocks when everyone else is. The time to get interested is when no one else is. You can't buy what is popular and do well."

"Be fearful when others are greedy and greedy only when others are fearful."

"The most important thing to do if you find yourself in a hole is to stop digging."

"Risk comes from not knowing what you're doing."

"Rule No. 1: never lose money; rule No. 2: don't forget rule No. 1"

"It's only when the tide goes out that you learn who has been swimming naked."

"Do not save what is left after spending; instead spend what is left after saving."

"If you buy things you do not need, soon you will have to sell things you need."

"Chains of habit are too light to be felt until they are too heavy to be broken."

"The most important investment you can make is in yourself."

"The difference between successful people and really successful people is that really successful people say no to almost everything."

"It's better to hang out with people better than you. Pick out associates whose behavior is better than yours and you'll drift in that direction."

"Tell me who your heroes are and I'll tell you how you'll turn out to be."

"It takes 20 years to build a reputation and five minutes to ruin it. If you think about that, you'll do things differently."

"Honesty is a very expensive gift, don't expect it from cheap people."

"Forecasts may tell you a great deal about the forecaster; they tell you nothing about the future."

"If past history was all that is needed to play the game of money, the richest people would be librarians."

"What the wise do in the beginning, fools do in the end."

"Games are won by players who focus on the playing field –- not by those whose eyes are glued to the scoreboard."

"It is easier to stay out of trouble than it is to get out of trouble"

Wall Street is the only place that people ride to in a Rolls Royce to get advice from those who take a subway"

"Wall street makes its money on activity and you make your money on inactivity"

"Price is what you pay. Value is what you get"

"To win, the first thing you have to do is not lose."

"People with pen do much bigger thefts than the people with guns."

"The stock market is a device for transferring money from the impatient to the patient"

Rakesh Jhunjhunwala quotes

*"If you cannot control your emotions,
you cannot control your money."*

*"Markets are like women - always mysterious, always
commanding, always uncertain and volatile."*

*"Make exit an independent decision,
not driven by profit or loss."*

*"Have conviction. Be patient. Your patience may
be tested, but your conviction will be rewarded."*

*"I have learnt two things about the press and
wives. When they say something – don't react."*

*"Have some cash in hand so that you can
grab the opportunity when it occurs."*

*"Give your investments time to mature. Be
Patient for the World to discover your gems."*

"As a rule in trading never ever average"

*"Prepare for losses. Losses are part and
parcel of stock market investor life."*

"If you see an opportunity, grab it today!"

"Learn from mistakes. Learn to take a loss."

"Always go against tide. Buy when others are selling and sell when others are buying."

Peter Lynch quotes

*"Behind every stock is a company.
Find out what it's doing"*

"Owning stocks is like having children -- don't get involved with more than you can handle."

"If you can't find any companies that you think are attractive, put your money in the bank until you discover some."

"Never invest in any idea you can't illustrate with a crayon."

"If a picture is worth a thousand words, in business, so is a number."

"The simpler it is, the better I like it."

"The natural-born investor is a myth."

Benjamin Graham quotes

"In the short run, the market is a voting machine, but in the long run it is a weighing machine."

"Investment is simple but not easy."

"A great company is not a great investment if you pay too much for the stock."

Brian Tracy

"It is the quality of time at work that counts and the quantity of time at home that matters."

"Long term thinking improves short term decision making."

"Six – P formula: Proper Prior Planning Prevents Poor Performance."

"Planning is bringing the future into the present so that you can do something about it now."

Philip Fisher quotes

"Forecasting is like trying to turn lead into gold."

"If an investor had bought at the absolute lows, it would have been more a matter of luck than anything else."

"Nothing is worth doing unless it is worth doing right."

"If you can't do a thing better than others are doing it, don't do it at all."

"Don't follow the crowd."

"Companies that have failed to go uphill have invariably gone downhill"

"The chief difference between a fool and a wise man is that the wise man learns from his mistakes, while the fool never does."

Stephen Covey quotes

"If the ladder is not leaning against the right wall, every step we take just gets us to the wrong place faster."

"To know and not to do is really not to know."

"The key is not to prioritize what's on your schedule, but to schedule your priorities."

"The proactive approach to a mistake is to acknowledge it instantly, correct and learn from it."

"If we keep doing what we're doing, we're going to keep getting what we're getting."

"If there is one thing certain in the business it's uncertainty."

SUGGESTED READING

All investors should cultivate the habit of reading. The following are some great books on investment.

- ✓ Common Stocks and Uncommon Profits by Phil Fisher.
- ✓ The Unusual Billionaires by Saurabh Mukherjea.
- ✓ The Warren Buffet Portfolio: Mastering the Power of the Focus Investment Strategy by Robert Hagstrom.
- ✓ Security Analysis by Graham and Dodd.
- ✓ The Intelligent Investor by Benjamin Graham.
- ✓ Tap Dancing to Work by Carol J Loomis.

Suggested websites for reference

www.moneycontrol.com
www.myiris.com
www.financialexpress.com
www.hindubusinessline.com

www.capitalideasonline.com
www.nseindia.com
www.bseindia.com
www.msei.in

STOCK MARKET TERMS

Bid - The buying price is called the bid price.

Offer - The selling price is called offer price.

Bid Quantity - The total number of shares available for buying is called bid quantity.

Offer Quantity - The total number of shares available for selling is called offer quantity.

Short selling - First selling and then buying is called short sell.

Limit Order - In limit order, the buying or selling price has to be mentioned and when the share price reaches the mentioned price, then the order will be executed.

Market Order - When you place buy or sell order at market rate, the market order gets immediately executed at the current available price.

Stop Loss Orders - Stop loss orders are used to stop or limit losses in the share market. The stop loss order is placed below the current market price of the stock to stop the loss in buy position; and above the current market price to stop the loss in short sell position.

Bull Phase - When the market keeps going up it is called the bull phase.

Bear Phase - When the market keeps going down it is called the bear phase.

Penny stock - Stock price less then Rs. 1 is called penny stock.

Large Cap stocks - Shares of those companies with a market capitalization of over Rs. 1000 crores are called large cap stocks.

Mid Cap stocks - Shares of those companies with market capitalization between Rs. 100 crores and Rs.1000 crores are called mid cap stocks

Small cap stocks - Shares of those companies with market capitalization of less then Rs. 100 crores are called small cap stocks

Upper Circuit - When the index or stock goes up by more than a fixed limit the exchange places the upper circuit for that stock or index. Trading is then suspended for some time to let the market cool down.

Upper circuit is a system lock used to stop excessive speculation in the stock market and is applied by the stock exchanges.

Lower Circuit - When the index or stock goes down by more than a fixed limit the exchange places the lower circuit for that stock or index.

The International Securities Identification Numbering (ISIN): ISIN has twelve alphanumeric characters and the sole purpose of ISIN is to number securities.

The first two digits denote the country of origin; the next nine characters are reserved for the unique identifying number for the security; the final digit is called a check digit that ensures the code's authenticity and prevents errors.

Example

ISIN of Reliance Industries Ltd. is IN E002A0101 8

IN - India
E - Company
002A - Company serial number
01 - Equity
01 - Issue number
8 - Check digit

Market capitalization - The value of a company is calculated by multiplying the total number of shares by the current share price.

Debt-to-Equity ratio - It is the ratio of total liabilities of a business to its shareholders' equity. To put it simply, it is a measure of the relationship between the capital contributed by creditors and the capital contributed by shareholders.

Price to earnings ratio indicates how cheap or expensive a stock is; in other words, how many times earnings they are willing to pay; this is calculated by dividing a company's total liabilities by its stockholders' equity.

Price to sale ratio - The P/S ratio measures the price of a company's stock against its annual sales, instead of earnings.

This is a more reliable ratio because sales are difficult to manipulate when compared to earnings.

P/S ratio = stock price/sales per share

Sales per share = (total revenue for twelve months/sales)/ Average shares outstanding

Price to book ratio - Calculated as:
P/B Ratio = Market Price per Share / Book Value per Share Where Book Value per Share = (Total Assets - Total Liabilities) / Number of shares outstanding

Good for evaluating bank stocks and companies with tangible assets.

Price-earnings ratio - The price-earnings ratio (P/E ratio) is the ratio for valuing a company that measures its current share price relative to its per-share earnings. The price-earnings ratio is also known as the price multiple or the earnings multiple.

The P/E ratio can be calculated as:

Market Value per Share / Earnings per Share (EPS)

EPS = (Net Income – Dividend if any) / Average Outstanding Shares

CAGR - The Compound Annual Growth Rate isn't a true return rate, it's rather a representational figure. It is essentially an imaginary number that describes the rate at which an investment would have grown if it had grown at a steady rate, which virtually never happens in reality.

To calculate compound annual growth rate, divide the value of an investment at the end of the period in question by its value at the beginning of that period, raise the result to the power of one divided by the period length, and subtract one from the subsequent result.

This can be written as follows:

Cagr = [(Ending value/Beginning value) ^ (1/no. of years)] -1

Peg ratio - The stock price (per share) of a company divided by its most recent twelve-month earnings per share is called its price-to-earnings ratio (P/E ratio). If this P/E ratio is then divided by expected earnings growth going forward, the result is called the price/earnings to growth ratio (PEG ratio).

Theoretical perfect correlation between market value and projected earnings growth assigns a PEG ratio value of 1 to a stock. PEG ratios higher than 1 are generally considered unfavorable, suggesting a stock is overvalued. Conversely, ratios lower than 1 are considered better, indicating that a stock is undervalued.

PEG= (P/E)/annual EPS growth

Valid till cancel order (VTC) - Using this feature you can place buy and sell limit orders in equity specifying the period for which you want the order instruction to be valid. The period selected by you should be within the maximum validity date defined by the broker.

After Market Orders (AMO) - After Market Order (AMO) feature helps you to place an order beyond the regular trading hours. This facility is provided to most of the customers who have an online trading account.

AMO is for those customers who are busy during market hours but wish to participate; simply put, your presence is not needed at the exchange to execute the order.

REFERENCE

Websites:

www.moneycontrol.com
http://www.nseindia.com
www.sebi.gov.in
https://nsdl.co.in
https://www.researchbytes.com
http://getricher.in
http://www.legalserviceindia.com
https://www.screener.in/screens
https://www.equitymaster.com
http://moneyexcel.com
https://www.brainyquote.com
http://www.charteredclub.com

Books:

- The Tao of Warren Buffet by Mary Buffet & David Clark.
- Buffetology by Mary Buffet.
- The Naked Trader by Robbie Burns.
- The Intelligent Investor by Benjamin Graham.
- NISM research analyst XV.
- One Upon The Wall Street by Peter Lynch.
- My Warren Buffet Bible by Robert L.Bloch.
- Warren Buffet and the Interpretation of Financial Statements by Mary Buffet & David Clark.

FINAL WORDS FROM THE AUTHOR

Dear Readers,

If you want to be financially free, then your income should be more than your expenses.

Financial freedom = income > expenses

Stock market is the best option available to attain financial freedom. Wish you all the very best. Happy investing!

I appreciate the trust that you have placed in me and I will continue to strive to provide you with quality service and guidance through www.equityforte.com Reviews are very important to any business, and I would love to get your insightful feedback and continue to deliver the best customer service.

I welcome unbiased and informative reviews. Feel free to write whatever you like; just for your convenience I have included a few questions that you can use as a guideline:

1. What prompted you to buy this book?
2. Share a specific feature that you most like about this book.
3. What benefit did you experience after reading this book?

Post your reviews at www.equityforte.com\testimonial or drop us an email at contact@equityforte.com. I appreciate your time and thank you once again for your business.

I look forward to hearing from you.

Best Regards,

Swaminathan Annamalai.

DON'T MISS OUT ON OUR EXCLUSIVE OFFER

Flat 15% off on our services at www.equityforte.com

Use coupon code – DIGITALSPACE4LIFE
to avail the offer

At equityforte.com our approach is straightforward - we create tangible value for your blocked investments. We are a one-stop shop for all your needs; be it dematerialization of shares, unclaimed dividends, selling delisted shares, reviewing existing portfolio as well as offering investment advice. Our service is custom designed and each case is thoroughly researched and the solutions offered are unique to each case.

Terms & conditions of the offer:

1) Coupons are intended for single use and only one promo code may be redeemed per user account.
2) Offer is applicable only when payment is done through payment gateway.
3) The Offer cannot be used in conjunction with any other offers.
4) We reserve the right to end the Offer or change the offer or to amend these terms and conditions at any time without prior notice.

www.ingramcontent.com/pod-product-compliance
Lightning Source LLC
Chambersburg PA
CBHW021542200526
45163CB00014B/728